FOXHUNTING

HOW TO WATCH AND LISTEN

THE DERRYDALE PRESS

FOXHUNTERS' LIBRARY

FOXHUNTING

HOW TO WATCH AND LISTEN

HUGH J. ROBARDS, MFH

Illustrations by Christine M. Cancelli

*With an Introduction by Norman Fine
Including Advice on Hunt Attire and Etiquette*

THE DERRYDALE PRESS
Lanham, New York, and Plymouth, UK

THE DERRYDALE PRESS

Published by The Derrydale Press
An imprint of The Rowman & Littlefield Publishing Group, Inc.
4501 Forbes Boulevard, Suite 200, Lanham, Maryland 20706
http://www.rlpgtrade.com

Estover Road, Plymouth PL6 7PY, United Kingdom

Distributed by National Book Network

British Library Cataloguing in Publication Information Available

The hardback edition of this book was previously cataloged by the
Library of Congress as follows:

Robards, Hugh, J.
Foxhunting : how to watch and listen / Hugh J. Robards.
p.   cm.
1. Fox hunting. I. Title.
SK284.R63 2006
799.2'59775—dc22
2005037246

ISBN 978-1-58667-120-4 (pbk. : alk. paper)
ISBN 978-1-58667-121-1 (electronic)

∞™ The paper used in this publication meets the minimum requirements of
American National Standard for Information Sciences—Permanence of
Paper for Printed Library Materials, ANSI/NISO Z39.48-1992.

CONTENTS

ACKNOWLEDGMENTS

I would like to thank my wife, Caroline, for doing all of the typing of my manuscript and for her encouragement. I thank Fritz Teroerde, M.F.H., for allowing the Chas Fagan print to be used on the dust cover and also Christine Cancelli for her excellent illustrations.

Special thanks must go to Jed Lyons, publisher of The Derrydale Press, and to editor Norman Fine, whose idea it was for me to write this book. I also thank Norman for writing the introduction and advice on hunting attire and etiquette, which I would have found far too complicated! Last but not least, I thank my very dear friend, Christian Hueber II, Joint-Master of the Radnor Hunt in Pennsylvania, for writing the foreword.

FOREWORD

I am privileged to have hunted in Ireland with Hugh Robards throughout the heyday of his years with the County Limerick Foxhounds. At that time motor traffic was almost nonexistent and bypass roads had not yet divided the country. Limerick was a foxhunter's paradise and the superb Old English pack was able to run unrestricted in any direction of the compass. Yet hunting hounds properly required much venery, as the drains with banks, hedges, or walls that bordered numerous small farms gave the hunted fox endless sporting chances to elude the pack. Further, it was not a straightforward job to stay with the hounds, as the country was far from easy to cross. Despite the challenges Hugh was seldom at a loss and continuously showed legendary sport to the Limerick subscribers and many international visitors.

Robards bred his Limerick hounds to a very high standard, and he hunted them with a panache that made the job look deceptively easy to the casual observer. Yet any field member who chose to watch Hugh Robards carefully could not miss the tremendous mental and physical energy he put into his work. For Hugh's success was based not just on innate talent and a love of hunting, but also on the disciplined thought and detailed preparation that he put into organizing every aspect of each hunting day.

In this book, Hugh Robards has made full use of his knowledge, passion, and forty-two years of experience to create a narrative that clearly and often humorously explains the art and the science of organized foxhunting in the field. His thoughts have been expressly written for the inquisitive field member in the interest of expanding his or her knowledge and enjoyment of hunting, but he achieves much more. For there are many ideas and observations that will also be of immense value to the experienced amateur or professional huntsman or whipper-in.

Hunting is a way of life for Hugh, which foxhunters are invited to share. In the second chapter he expertly pilots the reader through a very traditional and personal day of hunting as though they were riding right behind him. In each subsequent chapter, Hugh and the reader ride on the same hunt but from a totally different and interesting point of view. Correct interaction between the huntsman, the whippers-in, and hounds are clearly explained and should be required reading for anyone organizing a hunt. The fox receives proper respect as both a clever hunter and a wily quarry. The right way to be a good Field Master is carefully described from the perspective of one who knows they can be the huntsman's greatest friend or sometimes his worst nightmare. Often overlooked, the value of proper kennel management and consistent hound exercise are emphasized in a way that leaves the reader in no doubt about their importance in any hunting establishment.

Through firsthand knowledge, Hugh has been able to include detailed observations on the skills of great huntsmen, such as the Tenth Duke of Beaufort, the Second Lord Daresbury, and Captain Ronnie Wallace. Significantly, it is Hugh's own perceptive comments on hunting, especially his comparisons between venery on both sides of the Atlantic, that will give many foxhunters a broader understanding of their individual experiences and theories.

Those who missed the great hunting days in Ireland last century should know that Hugh Robards is now Joint-Master, along with Mrs. Armour N. Mellon, of the Rolling Rock Hunt in Ligonier, Pennsylvania. There he continues to hunt Old English hounds and provide truly exceptional sport.

Christian Hueber II, MFH
Indian Hill
Penn Valley, Pennsylvania

Note to the Reader

Definitions of foxhunting terms may be found in the glossary. The first use of these terms appears in italic throughout the text.

INTRODUCTION, INCLUDING ADVICE ON HUNTING ATTIRE AND ETIQUETTE

Follow Hugh Robards' fictitious huntsman as he hunts hounds over an interesting line of country dictated by the running fox. In each succeeding chapter, Robards takes us back over the very same country, each time from an altogether different viewpoint—that of the huntsman, the whipper-in, the Field Master, the hounds, and finally the fox.

Hugh Robards' purpose here is to help field members get more enjoyment from each hunting day by learning how to watch and listen to the huntsman, the whippers-in, and the hounds. What are they doing? Why are they doing it? What problems do they encounter? How do they overcome the problems? What can you learn by watching them?

Much of the drama of the hunt often unfolds while the field is standing still. Look around at your fellow field members. Many are chatting, patting (or cussing) their horses, adjusting tack, digging snacks from their pockets, or passing around a much-appreciated beverage. Mainly, they are impatiently waiting for something to happen so they can run and jump again.

These are the very moments, however, when the field member who knows what to look for, who can interpret the actions of the huntsman, the whipper-in, and the hounds, can reap a great deal more enjoyment from his or her hunting day. An experience I had a few years ago while visiting the Rolling Rock Hunt in Pennsylvania crystallized this notion for me.

Master and huntsman Hugh Robards had invited me to ride up with him and his hounds on this bright, crisp Saturday morning. Hounds had been drawing the woodland covert for a while, when suddenly Robards pointed with his horn to one hound. Seconds later that hound was the first to speak. Robards had seen a clue that something was about to happen. I had missed it.

"Good girl, Silver," he said warmly to the hound. Then to the pack, "Try on, my hearts!"

Hounds continued on toward a creek. Sterns started feathering and several more hounds began speaking tentatively.

"That's a curious line, isn't it?" muttered Robards to himself, watching his hounds closely, then gazing beyond them, left-handed.

To me, it was all random motion. Yet I had a flash of insight that, while I saw only where the fox *had been* by watching the hounds trailing, Robards saw where the fox *was going*. It seemed he could project the fox's perambulations ahead of hounds as if following a dotted line on a page. Sophisticated? Definitely. But it brought home to me very clearly that there was much to see if the eye were more educated.

Hugh Robards has drawn upon forty years of experiences—first whipping-in to some of the greatest English huntsmen of the last century, then hunting the renowned County Limerick foxhounds in Ireland—to give real-life examples of situations in the hunting field that the attentive and educated field member could have seen, heard, and understood had he or she been looking and listening. As with any worthwhile activity or passion, there is always more to learn. This book will set the reader on the path to a greater enjoyment of his or her foxhunting experience through a better understanding of what to look and listen for.

As a complement to Robards' more sophisticated text, the publisher has asked me to include information on two basic subjects that every foxhunter needs to know before entering the hunting field: hunt attire and hunt etiquette. Although this information is included for the benefit of the less experienced foxhunter, no one who has spent time in the hunting field can deny that confusion concerning correct attire and disregard for elements of etiquette persist among even experienced foxhunters!

HUNTING ATTIRE, TACK, AND APPOINTMENTS

The following suggestions for correct hunting attire have been extracted with permission from *Guidebook 1997*, a publication of the Masters of Foxhounds Association of North America, Berryville, Virginia (540-955-5680). Another authoritative and readily available reference is *Riding to Hounds in America* by William P. Wadsworth, MFH. This comprehensive and informative booklet was first published in 1962 by *The Chronicle of the Horse* and has been reprinted many times. Contact *The Chronicle of the Horse*, Middleburg, Virginia (540-687-6341).

A careful comparison of these—or indeed any other—resources will reveal differences in what is deemed correct attire. The fact is, there is no universal agreement regarding every detail of attire. However, a gentleman or lady rider who relies on any one these references may confidently appear in any hunting field in the country with assurance of being *correctly* or, at the very least, *acceptably* attired.

The hunting attire described here has, over the years, proved to be practical, comfortable and comparatively safe, for which reason it has become traditional. However, your Master has the authority to dictate the specific livery for your hunt or the degree of formality or informality of dress that suits your own particular country.

Master: Lady or Gentleman

- *Coat*: Square-cornered, single-breasted frock coat, cut to suit the wishes of the owner. No flaps on waistline, and no pockets on the outside of the coat except an optional whistle pocket. A Master who does not hunt hounds should have four front hunt buttons. A Master who does hunt hounds should have five buttons. There should also be two hunt buttons behind and two or three small buttons on the cuff of each sleeve. The material should be heavy twill or melton cloth. Scarlet (called "red" or "scarlet") is the most traditional color for hunting, but if the regular hunt livery is of another color, that color should be worn. The collar and lapels of hunt coats should be in conformity with the hunt's livery. No Master, whipper-in, huntsman or member should wear his or her hunt livery (scarlet coat, hunt colors or buttons) in another country unless invited to do so. It is correct to wear a black or dark coat when participating in a joint meet without their own hounds.
- *Breeches:* May be brown, rust, canary (ladies), buff or white, of heavy cord, heavy synthetic stretch twill, or other heavy material. Lightweight breeches of silk or light synthetic knits are not correct.
- *Vest:* Canary, tattersall, or appropriate hunt color.
- *Hat:* Black or dark blue (ladies) velvet hunting cap with ribbons down or up according to local custom. (Ribbons down traditionally indicate professional hunt staff.) A plain black safety helmet with chin harness securely fastened is recommended as well.

- **Boots:** Traditional hunting boots of black calf with brown tops sewn on, well polished, with tabs sewn on but not down. White or brown boot garters (to match breeches) may be worn. Rubber boots are acceptable, especially in wet weather.
- **Spurs:** Of heavy pattern with moderately short neck and no rowels. Light racing spurs are not permissible. Spurs should be set high on the boot just below the ankle and the spur arms should be parallel to the ground. The free end of the spur strap should be on top of or outside of the boot.
- **Gloves:** Heavy wash buff, brown, or black leather. White wool or string gloves are also acceptable.
- **Whip:** Traditional hunting whip.
- **Horn:** Traditional hunting horn carried in a leather case generally attached to the left-hand side of the saddle. *No horn should be carried by anyone except Master, huntsman, or first whipper-in when given permission by the Master.*
- **Wire Cutters:** Wire cutters may be carried in a leather case attached to the saddle.
- **Neckwear:** Plain hunting stock neatly tied and fastened with a plain, horizontal safety pin. Ends of the stock should be pinned down to remain tidy.
- **Flask and Sandwich Case:** Gentlemen may carry either a flask or sandwich case (or both). Ladies may carry either a sandwich case or a combination flask and sandwich case.

Honorary (Amateur) Huntsman

- **Turn-out:** The same as for Master. Should have five buttons on front of coat and ribbon on hat up or down, as determined by local custom.

Professional Huntsman

Same as Honorary Huntsman *except:*

- *Hat:* Ribbon down.
- *Couplings:* Should carry one set of couplings fastened to a D-ring on off-side of saddle.
- *Whip:* Traditional hunting whip or white whip and thong.
- *Flask and Sandwich case:* Not permitted.

Honorary Whipper-in

Same as Honorary Huntsman *except:*

- *Couplings:* Should carry one set of couplings fastened to a D-ring on off-side of saddle.

Professional Whipper-in

Same as Honorary Whipper-In *except*:

- *Flask and sandwich case:* Not permitted.
- *Coat:* Should have a large "hare pocket" on inside of skirt.
- *Stirrup leather:* Should be worn outside of coat over right shoulder, under left arm, buckled in front with the point of the strap down.
- *Hat:* Ribbon down.
- *Whip:* Regulation hunt whip or white whip and thong. If the huntsman carries a white whip and thong, the lash should be long enough to strike the ground.

Gentleman Member

- *Scarlet coat:* Should have rounded corners and three buttons in front, or:
- *Black coat:* Frock coat cut same as scarlet coat or black hunting coat is preferable to a shadbelly coat. Buttons may be regular buttons adopted by the hunt, but most preferably

a dark button with hunt initials or crest design in white. There should be three buttons on the front of the coat and two buttons on back if frock coat. It is not customary to wear Hunt colors on the collar of a black coat. It is customary that brass buttons on black coats are reserved for Masters, ex-Masters, honorary secretaries, and ex-honorary secretaries.

- *Vest:* Canary, tattersall, or appropriate color designated by the Master.
- *Breeches:* May be brown, rust, buff, or white (only with a frock coat), of heavy cord, heavy synthetic stretch twill, or other heavy material. Lightweight breeches of silk or synthetic knits are not correct.
- *Hat:* A safety helmet in black with chin harness fastened is recommended. Ribbon should be up. With the Master's permission, top hats can be worn with scarlet coat, frock coat, or shadbelly coat (hat-guard optional). Bowler hat with formal black hunting coat.
- *Boots:* Plain black calf without tops worn with black hunting coat. Brown-topped boots should be worn with frock coat. Black field boots with laces are not considered proper formal boots. White or brown boot garters (to match breeches) may be worn.
- *Hair:* If long, to be confined neatly.
- *Neckwear:* Plain white hunting stock neatly tied and fastened with a plain, *horizontal* safety pin. End of the stock should be pinned down to remain tidy.
- *Spurs:* Same as for Master.
- *Whip:* Traditional hunting whip.

Lady Member (Astride)

- *Coat:* Frock or hunting coat of black, dark blue, tan, dark gray, or dark-colored material, suitably cut, with buttons and collar trimming adopted by the hunt represented. Frock coat should have rounded corners with three buttons in front and two on back. Hunting coats have rounded corners and three buttons on the front of the coat.

- *Vest:* Canary, tattersall, or appropriate color designated by hunt.
- *Breeches:* Buff, rust, brown, or yellow (not white) cord or heavy synthetic stretch twill (not knitted) material.
- *Hat:* Velvet hunting cap in black or dark blue or a safety helmet in dark blue or black with a chin harness fastened is recommended. Ribbon up. With permission of the Master, black bowler or silk top hat (the crown should be six inches or more and worn only with a frock coat). Short dressage hats are not appropriate.
- ***Sandwich Case (or combination flask and sandwich case):*** Optional. Flask case is not customary.
- *Hair:* Should be neatly confined. Hair nets are advisable and correct.
- *Gloves:* Heavy wash leather, buff, black, or brown leather. White wool or cotton string gloves are allowed.
- *Spurs:* Regular hunting spurs, same as for Master.
- *Neckwear:* Plain white hunting stock neatly tied and fastened with a plain, horizontal safety pin. The ends should be pinned down to remain tidy. No other jewelry should be visible.
- *Whip:* Light hunting whip with thong.
- *Boots:* Black calf hunting boots without laces. Black leather or patent leather tops are appropriate, especially with a frock coat.

Lady Member (Side-Saddle)

Same as Lady Member (Astride) except:

- *Habit:* Dark melton or other cloth, suitably cut.
- *Veil:* Must be worn with a top hat but not with a bowler.

- *Hat:* Top silk (hunting hat) to be worn with double-breasted dress hunting coat (crown should be six inches). Black bowler (derby) to be worn with plain jackets. Safety headgear in black with chin harness properly fastened is recommended with ribbon up.

EXCEPTIONS

Juniors

It is not necessary for juniors to wear formal attire as it is often both difficult and expensive to obtain properly fitting formal attire in the small sizes. Whichever type of "turn out" is chosen, it should be immaculately clean and appropriate for various weather conditions with an approved ASTM (American Society of Testing Materials) safety helmet properly fastened.

Formal Attire

Same as for Lady Member (Astride). Junior colors may be worn according to individual hunt customs.

- *Hat:* A properly fitting ASTM-approved safety helmet with chin strap properly fastened is required with ribbon up.
- *Whip:* A lightweight hunting whip with or without thong.
- *Neckwear:* A plain white stock neatly tied and fastened with a plain, horizontal safety pin. Turtleneck shirts should not be worn except by very young children.
- *Hair:* If long, should be neatly confined or braided.

Informal Attire

- *Coat:* A tweed coat in a muted color (no scarlet).
- *Breeches:* Tan or brown breeches or jodhpurs.

- *Boots:* shined brown/black jodhpur boots.
- *Gloves:* string or brown/black leather.
- *Neckwear:* Plain or colored stock neatly tied and fastened with a plain, horizontal safety pin. "Ratcatcher" shirts are also correct with a neck band or neatly tied bow or man's necktie. Turtleneck shirts are usually for very young children only.
- *Hat:* As above.

In hunting countries where extremes of temperature regularly occur, modifications to the foregoing suggested formal attire may be in order. Such modifications for extremes of temperature may be made by the Master(s) of individual hunts as needed, particularly in cold weather when parkas and heavy jackets are very warm when worn over regular coats.

Gentlemen's and Ladies' Informal or Ratcatcher Attire

- *Hat:* Black hunting cap, black or brown bowler, or approved ASTM helmet with secure chin strap with ribbon up.
- *Coat:* Tweed or wool in muted color, tailored and vented
- *Shirt:* Ratcatcher or other light-colored shirt.
- *Neckwear:* Stock tie (plain or colored) with horizontal pin or man's necktie. Whether stock or necktie, ends should be pinned down to remain tidy. Neckbands are also appropriate for ladies. Turtlenecks and polo shirts are usually reserved for children, but are used in some hunts that experience extremely hot temperatures during cubhunting season.
- *Breeches:* Earth tone colors: buff, tan, grey, or rust.
- *Spurs:* Regular hunting style with no rowels.
- *Boots:* Brown or black leather, dress or field with laces. Formal boots with brown, patent, or leather tops are not appropriate. Rubber boots are acceptable with the Master's

permission as are canvas-topped (Newmarket) boots and jodhpur boots with either canvas or leather leggings.

- *Gloves:* Black or brown leather or string gloves.
- *Wire Cutters, Flask and Sandwich Case:* Same recommendations as in formal attire
- *Whip:* Regulation hunting whip. Thong and lash may be removed during cubhunting.

Lady Member (Side-Saddle)

- *Coat*: Beige, brown or off-white, suitably cut; plain, tweed, or salt sack.
- *Skirt*: Should coordinate with the coat.
- *Hat*: Bowler, velvet hunting cap, or safety helmet with chin harness fastened.
- *Veil*: Not appropriate for informal attire.

Accessories

- *Raincoats:* Masters can allow certain rain gear (common sense should prevail), but they should be used sparingly and be of muted colors (brown, black, or dark green).
- *Eye wear:* Sunglasses or tinted eye wear are not appropriate unless specifically prescribed or recommended by a physician. This does not preclude clear prescription glasses.

Tack

Horses and tack should be impeccably clean, polished, and shining. Anything less is a disservice to your hosts, the landowners.

- *Bridle:* Black or brown leather, may be either double or single. A caveson (noseband) should be used. Colored or ornamental brow bands are not acceptable.
- *Breastplate:* Optional.

- **Martingale:** Optional; if used, should be plain/raised leather. A running martingale must have "stops" on the reins.
- **Saddle:** Brown or black leather. Saddle pads (if used) should be saddle-shaped, of a light color (white, buff, or yellow). Numnahs or saddle cloths are not proper. Stirrup irons should be large, workman-like, and clean (shined). Safety equipment such as cruppers, grazing over-checks, and safety stirrups should be used whenever advisable.
- **Girth:** Preferably leather, but clean string and cloth girths are permissible as are girth covers made of fleece.
- **Accessories:** Accessories such as figure-eight and flash nosebands, bell and shin boots, gel and cushion saddle pads should be used sparingly and only when required for safety or health of the horse. Accessories like fly hood and ear or muzzle covers are not appropriate in the hunting field.

HUNTING ETIQUETTE

Why should we bother ourselves with the arcane etiquette of the hunting field? My answer is because we hunt for pleasure—a deeply satisfying pleasure at many levels—and it is infinitely more pleasurable to associate with people who are civil than with people who are cross.

All civilized societies adopt rules and conventions that allow individuals to interact without conflict. By the same token, unique activities, and especially activities involving a measure of risk (motor driving, sailing, foxhunting), develop of necessity their own unique rules and conventions that help assure a safe and pleasant outcome at the end of the day for all participants. Thus, the courtesies and conventions of the hunting field, developed over the centuries, aim to produce an environment in which the sport may flourish pleasurably and safely.

Landowners

If there is one single overarching concept to understand about foxhunting, it is that we are guests on someone's land and enjoy our sport solely through his or her goodwill. Without the landowner's hospitality, there is no hunting. The question is: How do we maintain that goodwill? We answer that question every hunting day in the way we treat our landowner's land, crops, and livestock.

- In general, commit no act that might test the landowner's goodwill.
- Greet the landowner cheerfully and respectfully if you should see him or her.
- Arrive at the meet early enough to get tacked up and mounted before hounds move off. The Master does not want latecomers straggling over the landowner's country, and the huntsman does not want latecomers heading the fox if it has circled back. If you are unavoidably late, stay to the roads after mounting up and wait for the best opportunity to join the field.
- All gates should be left as you find them. Closing a gate that was open might deprive livestock of their access to water. Leaving a gate open that was closed may allow livestock to escape or mix improperly with other stock. When in doubt, close the gate and tell the Field Master what you have done.
- If the field is passing through a gate, listen for the command as to what to do with the gate. If it is to be closed, you will hear, "Gate please." If it is to remain open, you may hear no command at all, but you may hear, "Gate open." In either case it is important that you acknowledge with a signal that you have heard the command. Likewise, if you are giving the command to those behind you, be certain your command is acknowledged. That is the only way to be certain the command was heard.

- If a gate is to be closed, it is the responsibility of the last one through to close it. It is common courtesy for one or two riders near the back to remain behind to help if necessary and to keep the gate closer's horse company.
- Never leave a gate for the second field or the hilltopping field to deal with unless they are close enough to acknowledge their understanding of what must be done.
- If a fence is damaged and cannot be repaired on the spot, advise the Field Master immediately so he or she can make appropriate and timely arrangements for its repair.
- Stay to the edge of all crop fields and seeded fields. If field members are crossing a pasture, it is best to spread out somewhat rather than erode a single track across the field.
- Slow down if livestock are running. Walk past dairy cattle. Walk past livestock during the calving, foaling, or lambing season. Do not ride between livestock and their offspring.
- Do not jump fences unnecessarily. You might break one and needlessly create a situation you have to resolve.
- Keep up with the field. If you are having difficulty keeping up, ask to be excused and fall back to the second field or the hilltopping field. Neither Master nor huntsman wants to see riders or small groups strung out across the country. The Master is concerned about the landowner, and the huntsman is concerned that if the fox doubles back it might be headed and the hunt spoiled.
- Unless you have specific personal permission, do not hack across private property on your own. Permission granted to the hunt does not bestow similar privileges on individual hunt members.
- Do not litter. Carry used food wrappers back home in your pocket.

- If you choose to leave the meet early, ask the Field Master if you may be excused and ask his advice regarding your route back to the meet. In general, you should hack back on the roads so as not to disturb any covert yet to be drawn.
- Do not sweep manure from your trailer at the meet. The landowner does not need your mess, nor should he have to wonder about your horse's deworming regimen.

Master and Staff

- The Master is the ultimate authority on any hunting day. His or her word is the law.
- Greet the Master politely upon arriving at the meet. Thank him and thank the staff at the end of the day. When departing, it is correct to say, "Goodnight," even if it's still morning!
- Don't talk to the huntsman during the hunt. His attention is and should be elsewhere.
- Never come between the huntsman and his hounds.
- Don't crowd the huntsman or his hounds.
- Don't pass the Field Master. Follow, but don't press. He is constantly revising his planned route based on how the hounds are running, what the huntsman is doing, and how the terrain is unfolding.
- Be quiet when the Field Master stops. He is listening for hounds.
- The whippers-in and the huntsman have the right of way. Always defer to them and allow them room to pass. When standing, always point your horse's head toward them as they pass.
- Never talk to a whipper-in during the hunt. His huntsman demands that he keeps his full attention on the hounds

and the quarry. Any distraction at the wrong moment that causes him to miss something he should have seen can irretrievably ruin a hunt.

Hounds and Quarry

- Hounds *always* have the right of way.
- The worst crime one can commit in the hunting field is to allow one's horse to kick a hound. You must do everything in your power to train your horse against this vice or punish your horse if he commits such a crime.
- Never ride ahead of hounds or ahead of the quarry. Never get between hounds and the quarry.
- When hounds are drawing for their quarry or casting after a check, remain still and quiet so as not to distract them.
- In general, never speak to a hound. That is the job of the huntsman and whippers-in.
- If hounds come near to you, turn your horse's head toward them.
- If you view a fox, never startle it with a "holloa." Its scent will change, and hounds will be confused. Wait quietly until it is some distance from you, then tell the Field Master what you have seen. Let the Field Master make the decision whether or not to holloa. If hounds are hunting well, the huntsman will not want to lift them and will not want them distracted.

Your Fellow Field Members

- Do not bring an unprepared horse into the hunting field. Of greater concern than the danger to yourself is the danger you pose to other innocents.
- If your horse is fractious or out of control, remove him from the hunt field immediately. Don't bring him back until you have solved his problems.

- If your horse kicks out at other horses occasionally, braid a red ribbon into his tail and keep him in the back of the field. If he cannot be cured of the vice, find another job for him away from the hunting field.
- If someone is riding too close behind, and you are afraid your horse may resent it, place one arm behind your back, forearm horizontal at the waist, palm out. This is a universal warning that your horse might kick. Likewise, if you see the rider in front give you such a signal, fall back.
- Do not allow your horse to nuzzle, nip, or rub the rump of the horse in front of you. Even a non-kicker can be provoked to kick.
- Do not coffee-house and chatter while hounds are hunting, even if you are far removed from the pack. It is annoying to other field members who are trying to watch and listen, and it is annoying to the huntsman when his hounds are distracted from their job.
- When warning other riders of holes or other hazards (i.e., "Ware hole," "Ware wire," etc.), turn and speak loudly enough to be heard only by the riders immediately behind you. Do not shout the warning so as to distract hounds. Point to the hazard with your whip, crop, or finger. If the warning has been repeated several times before you arrive at the hazard, and you think the people behind you are already alerted, it may only be necessary for you to point at it.
- When queued at a jump, be certain the rider in front of you is safely over before you jump.
- If your horse refuses a jump, go to the back and allow the other field members to jump ahead of you and go on. Everyone wants to keep up with hounds, and it is rude to prevent them from doing so if your horse is being obstinate.
- Before bringing a guest to your field, seek permission from your Master. If you bring a guest, introduce him to the Master as soon as possible. Your guest is your responsibility.

Acquaint him with any local protocol, and stay nearby to assist him.
- If you wish to visit another hunt, contact the hunt secretary to determine what you must do to receive permission to hunt.

Visiting

- It is not correct, when visiting another hunt, to wear the colors of your own hunt without the Master's permission or the Master's specific invitation to do so. Customarily, gentlemen and ladies wear black (also navy blue if a lady) frocks or regular hunting coats when visiting.
- Seek out the Master and introduce yourself as soon as possible.
- Seek out the field secretary and pay your capping fee. It is appreciated when your payment is enclosed in an envelope bearing your name and address.

I sincerely hope that the foregoing advice will prove to be valuable resource and reference information. Having got that behind you, and having schooled your horse to the point where you can pay less attention to it and more attention to hounds, turn the pages, and let Hugh Robards open your eyes and ears to a new level of awareness, appreciation, and joy in hunting. Finally, although Robards' text is intended primarily for the interested field member, I would be very surprised if aspiring (and even practicing) young huntsmen, whippers-in, or Field Masters did not pick up a useful idea or two as well.

Norman Fine
The Clearing
Millwood, Virginia

ONE

WHY DID THEY DO THAT?

Join us for a morning's hunt. Though fictitious, our hunt will include many episodes that take place during the course of a proper hunt—episodes which, if you have been hunting for even a short time, are typical of events you have seen in your own hunt field.

The hunt is the ultimate contest. Every episode or event that happens during a hunt poses a problem for one or more of the participants: huntsman, staff, hounds, or quarry. Every problem must be addressed quickly—rightly or wrongly. You have seen these problems arise, you have seen the players make the quick decisions, and you have often wondered why they did what they did.

If you have been baffled by events during the course of a hunt, you are not alone. I am often baffled, and I have been hunting hounds for more than thirty years. Let's take a quick look at this hunt we are about to have and identify some of the questions. Then, in the chapters to come, we'll follow each of the players individually over the same line of country—the huntsman, the whippers-in, the Field Master, the hounds, and, finally, the fox. We'll try to identify the problems confronted by each and examine the decisions they made. And I hope, when we come to the end of this day, you'll have a better notion of how to watch and listen to the huntsman, his staff, and the hounds and come away with a better understanding of the strategies behind their actions. I guarantee this will increase your enjoyment of each and every hunting day.

Even before the hounds move off you notice that both whippers-in have left the huntsman and the pack. Why did they leave before the hounds? Soon after, the huntsman leads his hounds to the first *draw* (where hounds are deployed to search for a fox). Why did he not blow his hunting horn on moving off, as you have heard other huntsman do?

As the huntsman puts the hounds into *covert* (woods or thick brush where the quarry might be found), you look around and wonder why the Field Master has stationed himself and the

Why did he not blow his hunting horn on moving off?

field in such a position. You heard the huntsman drawing the covert, but why, when he had got to the end, did he draw it back through again? As he came back through the covert you heard a hound *open* (speak). Was it wrong or was it right?

As the hounds leave the covert hunting with a good cry, you notice that the huntsman is not riding directly behind his hounds. Why not?

On approaching the road, the hounds *check* (lose the scent), then *cast* (deploy) themselves over. Why did the huntsman bring them back over the road when they checked? Why did he decide to cast his hounds left-handed up the road instead of right-handed? Why did the first whipper-in disappear up the road, and what has happened to the second whipper-in?

Hounds are running well once more and reach a small covert. You see deer going away on the other side, and hounds come out on their line. How does the huntsman know that his hounds are not hunting deer?

Continuing on at a slower pace, hounds reach a farm of arable land. Why does the huntsman not cast the hounds forward when they check? Which hounds are working out the line? Why does the Field Master, having brought the field to a halt, now walk slowly on, even though the pack is not running? What was the second whipper-in doing off his horse?

Getting away from the plough, hounds run a little sharper across some rough fields where you see the hounds divide as another fox jumps up. From out of nowhere the first whipper-in appears and stops one lot of hounds. How did he know which lot to stop?

Running on nicely across good country, the Field Master leads you over a couple of brooks. Why did he jump the brooks very close to a tree?

Why did the Field Master point out to you the six crows that appeared to be doing aerobatics two fields in front of the hounds? On reaching an estate wall, why did two hounds follow the huntsman instead of going over the wall with the rest of the pack?

You heard the *view holloa* (loud screech) of the first whipper-in. Why did the huntsman go to him so quickly? How did he know that it was not a fresh fox? Why did the huntsman pull up fifty yards away from the whipper-in, instead of taking the pack straight to where the fox had been seen?

Why, when the huntsman saw two hounds standing at the entrance to a drain, did he not cheer them on?

Slowly now, the hounds hunt on into a covert and you hear them *marking* (speaking, digging at the earth) to ground. You also hear the huntsman cheering them with his horn and voice. Why did the second whipper-in not go into the covert with the huntsman and the first whipper-in?

Why, on returning to his horse, did the huntsman badger the second whipper-in about counting the hounds?

These are questions that you may well ask during a hunting day. I hope you will discover the answers in the following chapters. Also I hope that you will continue to frame the questions and seek the answers to all aspects of the chase. If you do, foxhunting will remain forever fresh and challenging for you.

TWO

WHAT IS THE HUNTSMAN DOING?

The Rider I saw was a lean James Pigg,
Astride a Horse Rawboned and Big,
Blowing his Pied Pack over the Rocks,
On the Line of a Traveling Cheviot Fox.

—Will. H. Ogilvie

THE HUNTING PLAN

A day's hunting is, or should be, organized as well as a military maneuver. The Field Master will have been in contact with the Master to discuss any problems in the area, such as new seeds that have to be avoided or a landowner that has requested the hunt to keep out. The Field Master may well be familiar with the country to be hunted over, but it is always a good thing if he or she can walk the country the day before hunting. With modern-day farming methods the countryside is constantly changing.

The Master or huntsman will have sent out cards or made phone calls to all of the farmers over whose land he thinks he will be hunting. The wise huntsman will include all the farmers and landowners within a six-mile radius of the meet. If he produces a hunt with over a six-mile point from the meet, he will be quite happy the next day to placate any farmers he had not notified!

The Master will have met with the huntsman and discussed the draw for the day—the woods, coverts, rough ground, or likely places he will take hounds in search for a fox. Also discussed will be the areas to be avoided if possible, and, if such is the custom, the time and place that the second horses will be taken. It is essential that the huntsman has complete awareness of his draw and any landowner problems that he may encounter during the day. There is nothing worse for a huntsman than to arrive at the meet and be told that the draw has been changed. He has worried about the day all the night before, and to find that everything has been altered upsets his whole line of thinking.

Once he moves off from the meet he should have no interference from anyone. His mind should be on his hounds, hunting the fox, and showing sport to the field. During the course of the day he will be continually thinking, What are the hounds doing? What is the fox doing? Are his whippers-in in the correct place? Where should he go if he is getting through the draw too quickly? If he is into a good hunt he is thinking of where he can go and where he cannot go. His mind is on his job, and any interference is an unwanted distraction.

While hunting hounds he makes numerous decisions: what to do when hounds check, where to place his whippers- in, and whether information about the foxes that have been seen is of any value. A good huntsman should be decisive, and his decisions should be made quickly. If it is not the correct one, hard luck, but generally a quick man will make a correct quick decision. The huntsman must, at all times, be moving on with his hounds. A fox is a toddling creature; it keeps moving; and to *account* for it the huntsman must keep his hounds moving.

You, as a member of the field, may not have been aware of this preparation, but it is well for you to know some of the concerns that go on behind the scenes. When you arrive at the meet, which hopefully will be at least ten minutes before hounds move off, after paying your respects to the Master and hunt staff, you might run your eye over the pack. Is it the bitch pack or the dog hounds? Silly question, maybe. How many people that hunt care which pack they are riding behind?

Well, if you are really interested in hunting you should care. Some people think that the bitches hunt better that the dog hounds; others beg to differ. Nowadays very few packs can afford to hunt a dog pack and a bitch pack. Some hunt a bitch pack one day and a mixed pack (dogs and bitches) on another day. Generally it is only those packs that hunt four days a week that can indulge in the luxury of two packs. Lord Toby Daresbury's grandson, Johnny Greenall, used to hunt only bitches at the Meynell (UK), as does Nigel Peel at the North Cotswold (UK). This works well for both huntsmen, and they each show wonderful sport.

The late Captain Ronnie Wallace, when Master and huntsman of the Heythrop (UK, 1952–1977), always maintained that he could not get on with the dog hounds. Therefore the bitch pack came in for most of the work, but he still showed superb sport when he hunted the dog hounds. When I hunted the County Limerick Foxhounds (Ireland) four days a week, I hunted both the bitches and the dog hounds twice a week. Perhaps the only difference I found was that some days while hunting the bitches I thought the dog hounds may have done better and other days it may have been the other way round. On the whole I could not find a lot of difference in either pack. It is all very well saying that the bitches are sharper, but if well handled, dog hounds can be just as sharp, in my opinion. Yet there is no doubt that dog hounds will not be messed. If they feel that they are being made fools of, they will cock their legs and do very little. Perhaps this is why so many amateurs prefer to hunt a bitch pack and leave the dog hounds for the kennel huntsman to hunt on his days.

While you are admiring the hounds at the meet, try to count them. Don't be discouraged if it seems an impossible task. No, they'll never stand still for you. Try again the next hunting day. And the next. Your accuracy will improve! Don't forget that the hunt staff counts them in couples. Therefore, if you count sixteen couples there are thirty-two hounds standing around the huntsman's horse. If you are hunting with one of the packs in the Fell country of England, then you would count them individually. Why, I am not sure, but perhaps the Fell hound is more individualistic, does not run up in a pack as tightly as its lowland cousin over the rugged terrain it hunts, and is easier to count as an individual. Similarly, the lowland huntsman will talk of a *brace* of foxes or a *leash*, while the Fell huntsman will speak of two or three foxes.

When you are looking at the pack, try to pick out a couple of hounds that you think you will recognize during the day. This is not always an easy thing to do, particularly if you are hunting with a pack that has a uniform color. But every hound is differently marked as you will observe, that is if they are not all white. The renowned amateur huntsman Brian Fanshawe, when hunting the North Cotswold in the late 1970s, marked several of his hounds with blue spray so that he would recognize them in the field.

While you are doing this you will notice that the Master and huntsman are in conversation. This will not be idle conversation or the latest county gossip; this will be about the final plan of action for the day. Everything, as we have said, will have been prearranged, but there are always last-minute hiccups to straighten out. The Master may have had a late night call from a landowner who had some particular worry, and that information must be passed onto the huntsman.

Obviously the day's draw was discussed the day before hunting, but a great deal depends on the wind. Foxes run with the wind and the last thing a Master wants is to run through the day's draw in twenty minutes! How does that happen, you may wonder.

Considering the country to be hunted that day, if the huntsman draws his most upwind covert first, there is a real danger that the fox, running down the wind, will run through many of the other coverts that the huntsman had intended to draw. The Master and huntsman may discuss this at the meet, perhaps deciding to draw the covert first that is furthest downwind, thus lessening the chance of this happening. Great care goes into the planning of the draw.

Perhaps due to overnight rain the land may be wetter than it was expected to be, and there may be a large field in attendance. The Master may ask the huntsman to make delaying tactics, or to draw the biggest of the coverts first, hoping that a fox will hang about for a while and some of the field will eventually give the day up early and turn for home. You may not think this is an honest way to entertain subscribers, but without the landowners there would be no hunting. The Master is aware of this, and as he has been put into, or has put himself into, the thankless position of maintaining a hunting country that he hopes to pass on to the next Master in a healthy condition, he has to put his landowners first, even though he may take some flak from his members.

Captain Wallace was brilliant at looking after his landowners. He never forgot who came first. If he had, as he often did at the Heythrop, a huge field out on a Saturday—and when we say huge we are talking about a mounted field of three hundred—he would adopt delaying tactics. Not the type that leaves the field standing outside the covert shivering with the wet and cold while the huntsman chivvies a fox about inside in a lackluster way. No, the captain would somehow lead his field across every ploughed field in the country. His hounds may have been hunting, then again they may not, but they were always in front of him. On entering a large wood that he was aiming for, hounds would run around while many of the mounted field, thinking they had a good hunt, would head for home.

Once this had happened, the captain would gather up his hounds and turn to the vale where he would find a fox and give the remainder of the field a good hunt, still keeping his landowners happy. This is not artificial hunting. It may perhaps be tailoring the sport to the priority of the moment, but then how many professional huntsmen have tailored their efforts to their own priorities? They have not done it to keep the landowners happy; they have done it to keep the mounted field happy.

His hounds were always in front of him.

Arthur Thatcher, when professional huntsman to the Cottesmore at the turn of the twentieth century, was much admired by many people in the mounted field, but he was castigated by the future Master, the Fifth Lord Lonsdale (The Yellow Earl), in the manner he hunted his hounds. Field member Jimmy Finch, one of the best men to cross Leicestershire in Thatcher's time, was one of the very few that had hunted with Tom Firr, Frank Freeman and Arthur Thatcher. When asked his opinion of who was the best, his answer was, "You can never settle it, but I know whom I got most fun with, and that was dear old Arthur Thatcher!" However, it was Lonsdale's opinion that Thatcher galloped about too much. When his hounds were at fault he did not give them time to get their noses down. He was looking for the next covert to find a fox and be away again. This kept a large mounted field happily on the move, but it was not, in Lord Lonsdale's opinion, foxhunting.

Once when hunting the Limerick wall country, I felt that we had done quite enough in one area. It was still early in the day and we had run through all of the draw. There was still quite a large field out, so I had a problem. To get out of a mess I turned to the Field Master, told him that two hounds had got away in front, called for my hounds, jumped the biggest wall that I could see, which gave me a little space between myself and the field, and rode on over a nice line of walls, some of them quite tricky, to a corner of a field that held some gorse covert. I was in luck. It held a fox that continued taking me away from the morning's *foil* (the area of confused scents). The fox did not go far before it found an open hole. Playacting, I know, but the field had enjoyed a "four mile *point*"![1] I confess that was the only

1. A *point* is the longest distance in a straight line that may occur in a hunt. *As hounds ran*—the actual distance run—may be a lot further.

time I pulled such a stunt; there is always the risk of not finding a fox.

As a member of the field, you may not approve of either the captain's tactics, Arthur Thatcher's, or mine, but it must be remembered it was done and is done to keep either landowners or members of the field happy. If you are aware of what is going on you will take your time, save your horse, and be ready for the vale! This method has to be better than a committee-made decision backed by the chairman, who says that hounds will hunt, but the field may not leave the road. In that scenario, hounds meet, the chairman is mounted, nobody else comes out, and then he *demands* that the huntsman draw the vale!

DRAWING THE COVERT

You have observed the hounds at the meet and have a little insight into the goings-on between Master and huntsman now. On leaving the meet, you might want to keep close to the Field Master so you are in a good position to observe what is going on at the first draw. The whippers-in and other helpers have gone to various points of the covert to view the fox away. Notice, on approaching the covert, not one hound leaves the huntsman until he tells them to *leu in*, at which time hounds enter the covert and begin searching for the scent of a fox. If it is a large covert, the huntsman will draw it into the wind, thereby giving the pack every opportunity to wind and rouse their fox. He will also ride into the covert, cheering and encouraging his hounds: "Leu try, try in there, leu wind 'im, push 'im up, old dogs." That is what it looks like on paper, but most huntsmen make guttural noises that very few people can understand!

Most vocal terms used by the huntsman are corruptions of the hunting language brought to England by the Normans in 1066. "Leu in" is a corruption of "loup-in-there," which would translate to "wolf-in-there."

If the covert is thick in the bottom with rose briars and such, the huntsman will give his hounds plenty of time to draw. The more open parts will be drawn more quickly. In a large covert the huntsman will occasionally touch his horn (i.e., blow a short note). This will not only let the hounds that are drawing wide know where he is, but also his whippers-in and the Field Master.

If the covert to be drawn is small, then the huntsman will most probably draw it downwind. This will give the fox some warning and the chance to get up on his legs. The last thing a good huntsman wants to do with a big mounted field waiting for a gallop is to *chop* (kill) the fox in covert. You might notice that early in the season the huntsman may make quite a lot of noise while he is drawing for a fox, but as the season goes on, especially in a country that has been well hunted, he will not be as noisy. If he makes too much noise, foxes that have been well hunted in the past will be on their feet and gone.

Some huntsmen, when drawing a small covert late in the season, will send their whippers-in and spotters well on in advance. On approaching the covert the huntsman will blow a couple of notes on his horn without letting hounds into the covert. The fox, on hearing the horn, will be up and away. The whipper-in or spotter viewing the fox as it leaves the covert, signals to the huntsman either with his whistle or a *holloa* with his voice to let him know the fox has gone. The huntsman with all his hounds gallops to the place where the fox exited the covert. The whipper-in or spotter watches for any hounds that might take the *heel line* the wrong way, and the pack is away as one, hard on their fox. Charlie Wilkin, when hunting Sir Watkin William Wynn's hounds, was an artist at this technique, producing some very sharp bursts for the mounted field. This method worked too well for me once in Limerick. I put the pack onto the line and that was the last we saw of them for an hour!

Again, huntsmen differ in this respect. Some like to get their hounds away close to the fox so that the fox does not have time to empty himself, believing that, particularly on a good scenting day, the field will enjoy a quick burst of twenty minutes over a good line of country. Other huntsmen believe that if a fox has a good start, it will provide a hunt with a long point.

Remember, foxes can be found in all kinds of strange places, such as willow trees and automobile junkyards. They love to lie up in the ivy on derelict buildings or high walls. If the weather is mild, they may well lie out in the open and even in a furrow of a ploughed field.

You will notice that when the huntsman is drawing an open area such as a ploughed field, he will keep one of his whippers-in close by to stop the hounds from catching the fox before it gets on its feet. Foxes that lie in the open are inclined to leave it to the last moment before they get to their feet. Foxes know that while they are lying tight they are not producing any scent and hounds may pass them by. This is common with all wildlife.

Often a covert will be drawn *blank* when it has actually held a fox. I had drawn a covert in Limerick blank and was hacking up the road to the next draw when a very nice man caught me up on his bicycle and told me that I had left the fox behind. He had just seen it go away! He very kindly led me back to where he had seen the fox, and a good hunt was enjoyed. Better to be born lucky than rich!

An observant huntsman will watch his hounds all the time while they are drawing, looking for signs of a fox being about. If you have remained close to the Field Master, you might do the same. Both you and the huntsman might see an old hound with his nose well down searching every leaf and log. He is doing everything he can to say that a fox is or has been there. The huntsman will see that this hound is frustrated; he wants to throw his tongue but will not in case he is wrong. This is where the huntsman can help. He has watched the hound work yet come up with nothing. Now the huntsman must work with this hound. He too must start searching for the fox. The hound has shown him that there has been one about and now, with the rest of the pack, every nook and cranny of the covert must be investigated. It is detective work, which should result in a find.

He has worked through the covert without finding, and has not heard a *holloa* from the whipper-in. Yet he is sure there is a fox there because his hounds have in their own way told him. As this is the first covert drawn, the huntsman has no idea yet of the scenting conditions—whether good, bad, or indifferent. He does not know if it is the *drag* (line) of a fox that has passed through the covert in the night. The huntsman has to use his instinct and his woodcraft. He also has to know his hounds. This is something you as a member of the field may not observe unless you are standing in a large woodland or looking down at the hounds from a height as they work below you.

On reaching the end of the covert, he once again touches his horn and calls, *"Elope, e'lou,"* or *"try bike,"* which is an instruction for his hounds to turn with him, and once again draw through the covert, not forgetting that this time they do not have the advantage of the wind. The huntsman knows this and will try to get his hounds to tack the wind, that is, draw across it as a sailor would do when sailing a yacht. In other words, making the most of the wind in the hope the hounds will wind the fox, the huntsman now has the pack quartering the ground in much the same way as a shooter would have his pointer or setter work for him.

THE FIND

Try to position yourself so that you can hear what the huntsman is doing. Hopefully, you have heard him turn back in the coyert as has the Field Master. Your hunt is fortunate if it has a Field Master who does not tolerate a lot of chatter—one who believes, as did the ancient Greeks, that talking out hunting is unlucky. If you listen you may hear a hound whimper. The huntsman has not only heard, but has seen Wagtail trying to take a line to the edge of the covert where some thick briars cover the boundary ditch. The pack also heard the whimper and, knowing it is Wagtail, a hound on whose opinion they can rely, have come in close to her and the huntsman. Now you may see the huntsman quietly edge his hounds toward the ditch. As you strain to hear what is going on, everything in the covert has fallen silent.

All at once there is a huge roar of hound music as the pack rouses the fox in the boundary ditch. All of the mounted field are now tense in their saddles waiting for the hoped-for *holloa* from a whipper-in, letting the huntsman and the world know that the fox has fled the covert. It does not happen. Once again there is silence. The pack was too close to its quarry and the fox has turned short back into the covert. You must now realize that hounds have drawn the covert twice, it is badly foiled by their own tracks as well as the fox's, and the fox takes full advantage of this to gain some respite from the hounds. You will notice that the huntsman is still silent. All he wants is for his hounds to keep their heads down and keep trying for the scent of the fox over the foiled ground.[2]

2. Foil is a term used when the ground that the hounds are hunting over has been tainted by the smell of cattle, deer, sheep, or other livestock, animals other than the quarry, smoke, or exhaust fumes from vehicles. All types of manure are also considered foil. In this case, the hounds have foiled the covert with their own scent.

This has not been a copybook find for the huntsman, but he must now keep his head and his mind on the job at hand, difficult as it is. His hounds are working hard over the foiled ground. Their sterns start to wave, and then the hound Villager opens. The pack clusters around him and, as one, opens on the line of the fox. What a glorious noise they make as they now get close to their quarry. The huntsman, as you note, is still quiet, the hounds are making all the noise that is necessary as they ring the covert.

Once again the mounted field becomes tense. Then, much to the Field Master's relief, there comes a shrill *view halloa* from the far side of the covert, but still he holds the field steady. You will hear the huntsman cheering the pack to the holloa: "Forrard, forrard, forrard." Still no need to use his horn as the hounds are packed up and driving on. Normally the huntsman would not cheer the pack to the holloa in case they were hunting another fox, but as he has drawn the covert twice, he is certain that there is only one. Perhaps, as the pack is running so well, it is unnecessary for him to cheer them, but it does let the whipper-in know that his holloa has been heard. The pack has now reached the whipper-in, who is standing just a little away from the line of the fox, with his horse's head and his hunting cap pointing in the direction the fox has gone.

Now at last, as the pack settles to the line, you will hear the long and exciting notes of the *gone away*. Tighten your girth, sit down in the saddle, and plan to ride as close to the Field Master as you can. Look forward to taking those glorious fences as they come, but remain observant! We have already decided that there is more to foxhunting than crossing country, so let us now sit back quietly, take our time, and observe what the huntsman is doing.

The huntsman was somewhat relieved to hear the whipper-in letting him know that he has counted hounds away as they

The whipper-in has his horse's head and his hunt cap
pointing in the direction the fox has gone.

came out of the covert and that they are all there. As he passes
his whipper-in, he hears, "*All on*, sir." As you watch the huntsman crossing country behind his hounds, you may think he is
the luckiest man in the world: to be mounted on a good horse
and paid to do a job he thoroughly enjoys. Perhaps he is a lucky
man, but the huntsman is aware that to many people he is only
as good as his last hunt. As Mr. Jorrocks would say, "A fish fag's
ware isn't more perishable than an 'untsman's fame."

As we mentioned before, the huntsman's mind is focused
on the job at hand. He does not ride for reputation; he rides
to keep with his hounds. He may have a second horse, but he
rides the first one as if he is not getting a second. Therefore,
he has necessarily developed an eye for a country, picking
the place to jump in a fence with an experienced eye. He is
also looking ahead, trying to divine the fox's destination. Is it

some woodland stronghold, or is it a head of open *earths*? Is the fox inclined to be bearing to the left or to the right?

These observations will help influence him in his casts if he has to help the pack at a check. His thoughts are also on the things that may cause the pack to check: a herd of cattle on the side of the hill that the fox is pointing for; that heavy shower of rain that is threatening to fall and obliterate the scent; and, perhaps the worst of all, the farm laborer burning hedge trimmings. The fox is running downwind, the smoke is drifting downwind, the huntsman is making a mental calculation of how far he will have to take the pack on if they check in the smoke. You must not forget that even when he has got the pack beyond the smoke, it takes time for their noses to clear from the smoke. The same problem is caused by the exhaust fumes from automobiles.

The huntsman not only has these things to think about, but as you noticed at the meet, he was in deep conversation with the Master. There was a problem. A landowner had telephoned the Master quite late the night before the meet asking that hounds not enter his lands as he was having his cattle tested the day of the meet. This property is smack in the middle of the day's draw. The landowner has always welcomed the hunt, and he is the last person in the world that the Master and huntsman would like to fall out with. So, as you can imagine, the huntsman is under quite a lot of pressure. He wants to keep the mounted field happy and produce a good hunt, but he also wants to protect the landowner.

THE RUN

Notice that the huntsman is not riding directly behind his hounds. He rides a little to the side of them so as not to unwittingly push the pack over the line if the fox makes a turn.

Also, if they come to a check they will have room to try back for themselves.

If you are well mounted and able to observe what is going on in front, you may see that the hounds have reached a road and, on crossing it, have stopped speaking. They fan out, some hounds coming back to the road. The Field Master stands well back from the check. It is a country road with no traffic, but could a car have gone down the road and *headed* (changed the course of) the fox? Watching, you may see the huntsman quietly bring the pack back to the field before the road just in case this has happened. Once again the pack fans out, but no hound opens.

You would have had to be paying particular attention to have noticed that the pack approached the road slightly at an angle to the left before they stopped speaking. Your huntsman noticed. This is why he now takes his hounds left-handed up the road. Believe it or not, one of the hounds that you picked out at the meet has started *feathering* (waving its stern) up the center of the road. The huntsman says nothing, but slowly walks behind the pack. The next thing you hear is your hound speaking. The rest of the hounds go to her but cannot *honor* her (by speaking to the line). You will notice that the huntsman is not pressing his pack on. He knows that sometimes the hounds with the capability of hunting the line up a road, when pressed, can go beyond where the fox turned off. This is the case now as you see your hound go on, but the pack suddenly surges to the right and once again is in *full cry*.

A hound that can take the line of a fox up a road is a huge bonus to any pack. The best hound I ever saw with this trait was Limerick Lincoln '68. Once during a good hunt late in the afternoon, hounds checked on a very quiet country road. Lincoln took the line of the fox for half a mile along the road to a crossroads, throwing his tongue all the way. On reaching the cross, he turned right, ran the road for another two hundred yards and then turned left-handed through the fence where the rest of the pack joined him. On another occasion he ran a road for a good quarter of a mile passing a man on a bicycle. I thought he must be having me on, as no fox would have passed the man, but upon inquiring I discovered that the man had only just come onto the road out of a cottage. The pack on leaving the road once again went on and accounted for their fox.

Again our pack is running well but pointing for a small covert a couple of fields away. For some reason neither of the whippers-in are there to view the fox away. As hounds enter the covert you notice six deer going away on the other side. The covert being small, hounds are quickly through it and come out on the same side as the deer, which causes a check. The huntsman also saw the deer go away, and he is a little

Lincoln ran the road for a quarter of a mile, passing a man on a bicycle.
I thought he was having me on.

concerned when a couple of young hounds start to speak, but he does not interfere with them. As you watch you notice the young hounds have stopped speaking, several other hounds have gone with their noses down to where the young hounds last spoke, one of them starts feathering, rushes forward and opens. This is one of the huntsman's most trusted hounds. You can almost tell his feeling for this hound in his cheer to the rest of the pack, and his relief when once again the pack is *running with a good head* (running up together).

This may appear to you, an observer, a not too serious check, but no matter how much a huntsman trusts his hounds, under these circumstances there is always that slight shadow of doubt in his mind. In this instance the huntsman does not know if the fox went in front of the deer or if it came out behind the deer. It was impossible for him to cast his hounds or interfere with them as the fox may even have been running with the deer. Therefore he has to rely on his old hounds, yet he will take note of the couple of young hounds that opened first. They may well have been correct.

Many times a hare will run through the same *smeus* in a fence that a fox has already gone through, causing the casual observer to assume that the pack is rioting on the hare. Some huntsmen may do nothing about hounds rioting on hare if they think there is the chance of the pack changing onto fox. Obviously this does not happen during the course of a hunt, but it may happen if hounds have not found a fox.

During Captain Wallace's Mastership at the Heythrop, he would take the bitch pack down to Exmoor to hunt through April. He would send his kennel-huntsman on in advance with that pack while he hunted the dog hounds for the last day in the Heythrop country. As the kennel-huntsman was absent, he would invite a professional huntsman from one of the packs close by to whip-in to him. One year he invited Jim Bennett, a famous huntsman through the latter half of the twentieth century of the Old Berkeley and later the Vale of Aylesbury. Jim made the big mistake of telling the captain that his hounds were hunting hare. He received such a dressing down that he never hunted with the captain again. Jim was probably correct, but the captain did not always want to know these things.

Once when hunting hounds on foot (unmounted) in Connemara, the small pack that I had out was running hard beside a stone wall with four lambs running a hound's length in front of them. You can imagine my relief when the pack turned right, jumped the wall, and continued on with the fox!

This check has given our fox a little leeway and the pack is now finding it more difficult to hold the line. Frustrating for the huntsman and not helped by the fact that the fox has run onto some ploughed land. If it had just been one ploughed field, the huntsman may have got hold of his hounds, taken them across the plough, and cast them on. But they are now on an arable farm with plough land of over a hundred acres. Sad for the huntsman, but good for you, as you can now watch hounds steadily working the line. This is now where the *low scenting* hounds come into play, or as some huntsmen refer to them, "hounds with *cold noses.*" Generally these are older hounds. You will notice these hounds, heads down, working every inch of the line, not continuously speaking, but every now and then opening to let the rest of the pack know that they still have the quarry in their olfactory sights.

Perhaps on the headland of the plough beside the fence the rest of the pack will honor them, only for the cry to die again as they enter the next field of plough. The huntsman at this stage will have a good idea of the direction the fox is taking and you will notice that he is quietly moving his pack on. Some huntsman when casting their hounds will encourage them with the words, "yut, yut, yut." Others whistle softly.

Your huntsman is being quiet, watching every hound but moving on. The hounds still have their heads down, but they also are going forward.

Watching, you will notice that the huntsman moves the pack a little faster as he sees that there are some rough fields beyond the plough. Why does he move faster? Well, he hopes that once he gets the pack off the plough, scent may be a little better on the grass. The huntsman has read the line correctly. Once the pack reaches the grass, first one hound opens, then another, and once again the pack is hunting as a unit.

The deer episode delayed hounds and the plough has also helped the fox to get a good lead, but you will notice that the air has become a little cooler. You are aware that the pack is running faster because you have now got to sharpen up to keep with the Field Master. The going is better over the rough fields, as it is drier, being uncultivated old turf. What you do not know is that these rough fields, being dry and sheltered from the wind, make ideal laying for foxes, and it is just as he is coming to the end of these fields that the huntsman meets his next problem.

You saw a fox jump up in front of the pack. Perhaps you thought it was the hunted one, but the huntsman knows better. Luckily the first whipper-in riding on the downwind side of the pack has also seen what happened and gets to the head of the main body and turns them back to three couples of hounds that are still hunting the line of the original fox. This episode with a fresh fox was easy to overcome, as the huntsman and whipper-in were aware of what happened, and it was corrected with very little delay.

At another time the pack might have hunted on with the fresh fox, but the huntsman would notice that the lead hounds had dropped back and others would have taken their place. He may be lucky to be in a position to see exactly when this happened, therefore having some idea of how to correct the pack when the whipper-in has got them stopped. If he is not there to see the lead hounds drop back he has a problem.

When the pack divided, life became easier for the huntsman, as it is generally accepted that the smaller lot of hounds will stay with the hunted fox. Some huntsmen are lucky to have maybe one or two hounds that will not change foxes. Limerick Lancer was a fine example of this type of hound. If the pack changed onto a fresh fox, he would wait for them to be stopped and then continue on. He did this once when I was by myself with hounds. Luckily the main body, once they had changed, soon marked to ground and I was quickly able to get them back to Lancer and eventually complete a four-mile point.

This incident has now passed, and you are pleased to see that hounds are running well into open country. But beyond is a quite large property with an estate wall around it. On reaching the wall you are amazed at the way the hounds scale such an obstacle with hardly any hesitation. Perhaps the pack is aware that the fox is not far in front. Through the center of this property is a river which causes the pack to check. You watch as some hounds try to the left and others to the right, but you also see one hound who has taken to the water with a couple of others, and you notice as he swims that he is trying for the fox's scent on the lily pads. Halfway across the river he gets the scent and opens. The rest of the pack joins him and now you and the rest of the field have to quickly get to the bridge, which is close by. On reaching the other side of the river you see that the pack has once again checked. The fox is tiring, which means he is not leaving as much scent. Also the water dripping off him has helped to dilute the scent. Every hound has its nose down working hard to recover the line. You notice that the huntsman is standing back letting them work. If the truth is known, the huntsman is at a loss as to what the fox has done. Perhaps he was thinking that the fox had not come out of the river where the hounds had, but had drifted down river with the current. Then you hear a shrill *view holloa*.

The first whipper-in has got well on downwind and viewed the hunted fox out of the demesne via a hole in the wall. The huntsman, knowing that his whipper-in would never holloa him onto a fresh fox, quickly gets hold of his hounds by doubling his horn (short quick notes), and gallops to the holloa. The whipper-in is standing pointing his cap in the direction the fox has gone into a hedgerow. Fifty yards before the whipper-in, the huntsman pulls up and encourages the pack into the hedge. You may wonder why he did this—why did he not take the pack straight up to the whipper-in? By stopping short of the hedge, the huntsman reduced the chance of the pack taking the heel line. For some reason when there is little scent, hounds are more prone to hunt the heel line. By keeping the pack between himself and the fox he can prevent this happening. Also the first whipper-in is aware of this problem, and you will notice that he also has moved into a position to prevent it.

This time all is well. The pack does not open with a great cry, but every hound is working. They go through the hedge but in their haste overshoot the line. The fox is now tired and has turned short back down the hedge. The huntsman stands still and lets the hounds come back by themselves. At first nothing happens, then there is a burst of music as the pack screams down the hedge knowing that the fox is close. You see that both whippers-in are at the bottom of the fence, one on each side. The Field Master holds you steady. Now is not the time to move and foil the line with sweaty horses. Sweating horses, bonfire smoke, and exhaust fumes from cars are the worst types of foil a huntsman has to deal with.

Every hound is on the left-hand side of the hedge and the huntsman is on the opposite side. Then like a flash you see the fox dart away in between the huntsman and the second whipper-in to disappear into some rough ground. Hounds come out of the hedgerow at top pace and reach the place that the fox was last seen and come to a halt. As the fox left the hedgerow you saw both of the whippers-in once more disappear into the country.

MARKING TO GROUND

Again the huntsman stands back and watches the pack cast themselves. As he watches, you also notice what he has seen: two hounds are standing at the entrance to a drain. They are not marking but they are taking a lot of interest in it. The huntsman does not encourage these hounds. Instead he quietly moves the rest of the pack beyond them. You notice several hounds moving a little quicker, then one, then another opens, and the two that were at the drain join the rest of the pack. Hunting on quite slowly now the pack reaches a small covert. You see that both whippers-in are already positioned each side of it. As hounds enter the covert the cry ceases for a couple of minutes and then you hear their deep frantic *baying* as they mark their fox to ground.

The long notes of the huntsman's horn blows "gone to ground." He also cheers his hounds: "Leu in, leu in, leu in, wind 'im, who-whoop, wind 'im in there." This has been a difficult hunt for the huntsman, and no doubt he is delighted that his hounds have marked their fox to ground, although disappointed that they did not catch it in the hedgerow. For you it has been an interesting hunt, and in a short space of time you have learned a little about hound work and some of the problems the huntsman must overcome.

Unfortunately for the huntsman, no matter how brilliant he is, not all hunts end with hounds accounting for their fox by either marking it to ground or catching it. So now while you are hacking home after quite a useful hunt, try and think back to previous days during the season when hounds have run well but still have not accounted for their foxes. Why do hounds lose their foxes? This question might flit through your mind and be quickly forgotten, but it nags at a conscientious huntsman and often wakes him in the middle of the night.

FOIL

You might recall a day in November, not long after the opening meet, when hounds had met in your favorite part of the country. It was a good hunt, hounds had run well, you were riding your old favorite, and so you were well up when hounds checked in the sheep. You saw the shepherd's dog coming back from your left, but did not realize he was the cause of the trouble. The huntsman, seeing where hounds entered the sheep, took them on, hoping to hit the line, but did not. He cast all round the field, but nothing. He did not know that the shepherd's dog had viewed the fox coming out of the sheep and chased it back the way it had come. A hopeless check—a lifesaver for the fox. Not only had the sheep foiled the scent but the dog did as well.

Even if the huntsman had seen the dog when you did, he would not have realized that it had ruined the hunt, as it came back running beside the field. That same day, which must have been a nightmare for the huntsman, the second fox ran onto the ground that had been foiled by the horses in the first hunt and eluded the pack. This is one of the most common ways of losing a fox.

BAD DECISIONS; GOOD DECISIONS

Then there was the day visiting a neighboring hunt. Admittedly there was not a great deal of scent, but you would have noticed how noisy the huntsman was, forever blowing his horn and galloping about. His hounds never had the chance to settle and get their heads down. Instead of taking them through gateways to a holloa, he jumped the biggest fences he could find so that when he got up to where the fox had been viewed his hounds were strung out over three fields struggling to get through the hedges.

Yet there were other days when you were fascinated by certain things that a huntsman did to regain the line of the fox, or a certain maneuver that helped to produce a hunt. Like that foggy day when the Master gave the order to move off, perhaps a little too quickly. You could only just see the length of two fields when hounds drew the first covert. Hounds quickly found, ran around the covert once and marked to ground. You were astonished that the huntsman did not allow his hounds to delay at the earth. Instead he came quickly out of the covert with the pack, back onto the road and hurried on down it. It was thought that he was in bad humor! But a mile down the road he cheered his hounds through a fence line. The pack settled to their task with a roar of music producing a good hunt and a fox caught in the open.

It transpired later that while the pack was hunting in the covert the huntsman had observed a couple of hounds disappearing into the fog. There was just a chance that if he was quick enough he might be able to get the rest of the pack onto them. It was a huge gamble but it paid off. Lucky, yes, but it is this type of maneuver that makes a huntsman's reputation. If it had not worked, well, that would have been another matter!

Another day comes to your mind. Once again into a super hunt the pack was running top pace when it checked beside a road. On this occasion you noticed that as soon as the pack checked, without any hesitation the huntsman got hold of them and took them back two fields the way they had come. Once back to a certain spot, he stopped, turned his horse to the left and hounds were away like lightning. You were so taken by this maneuver that at the end of the day you waited for your moment to ask the huntsman how he knew what to do so quickly at this check.

His response was almost as quick as his cast. He explained that he took the hounds back to that point because, when they passed that way toward the road he saw a very good bitch turn in the middle of the pack and hesitate, but once she saw the pack go on she went on with them to the check.

You must remember when questioning the huntsman that he may not always be able to tell you exactly why he made a certain cast. Many times it is what one may call a "gut feeling." For example, when drawing a favorite gorse covert a couple of weeks ago that is generally a certain find, you watched as the huntsman finished drawing it blank, and instead of coming out the usual way he let his hounds wander across the field to a small patch of briars beside a wall where they immediately roused a fox. Not only do the hounds have to get tuned into the scenting conditions during a day's hunting, but the huntsman also has to get tuned into his hounds. He has to become part of the pack. This takes a considerable amount of concentration. That is why huntsmen do not usually like people riding in their pocket. Even when drawing a covert he is watching his hounds for any little sign that will show him that a fox has been about and listening for the slightest whimper. To quote Jorrocks, "None but an 'untsman knows an 'untsman's cares."

THREE

WHAT IS THE WHIPPER-IN DOING?

'Oh,' gathering 'Ounds is the Job I Love,
W'en the Dark comes down on the Thorn,
An' the Moon is 'ung in the Sky Above,
Like a Glitterin' 'Untin 'Orn.

—Will. H. Ogilvie

AT THE MEET

Having talked about the huntsman, now let us go back to the meet and follow the whipper-in over the same line of country. Some huntsmen are vain enough to say they do not require a whipper-in. Such vanity is foolish! A moderate huntsman will catch more foxes with a brilliant whipper-in then a brilliant huntsman with a moderate whipper-in.

You have seen both whippers-in working with your home pack, and you have heard recently that this is the last season that the first whipper-in will be with this pack. He has worked his way up the ladder, starting his career as a kennel boy, then moving into the hunt stables as a second horseman. From there he moved on after a couple of seasons to become a second whipper-in to a four-day-a-week pack. Three seasons later he took the first whipper-in's position to a well-known two-day-a-week pack, where he stayed for two seasons before arriving as first whipper-in with your hunt. He has been with you for three seasons. On several occasions he has shown good sport when carrying the horn in the huntsman's absence. Your huntsman will miss him, but the whipper-in has achieved his goal. He has been offered the position of huntsman in a good country with a top class pack of hounds, which he deserves.

The second whipper-in is in his first season, an enthusiastic youth who started his career in the hunt stables. He is just starting to realize that hunt service is not all "scarlet coat and white breeches"!

Both whippers-in stand, one on each side of the pack, in silence, neither of them taking their eyes off the hounds except to touch their caps to say "good morning" in reply to greetings from field members. You greet both of them, but do not indulge in conversation. Like the huntsman, their minds have to be totally on the job at hand.

The first whipper-in knows the plan of action. He is experienced, he does not have to be told the draw, he can almost read the huntsman's mind by now. You will notice during the day that he never comes up from behind. You may not see much of him, but when he is required to assist the huntsman he appears almost by magic. The only thing the huntsman talks to him about at the meet is the landowner that does not want the hounds on his property.

There is somewhat more conversation between the huntsman and the second whipper-in. The huntsman has just corrected him for holding his whip in the wrong hand. Standing on the left of the pack, he should have his whip in his left hand. The whip should always be on the opposite side of his horse from the hounds. By way of illustration, refer to *The Chase* by

Michael Clayton. Of the six pictures of whippers-in, not one carries his whip in the wrong hand!

The huntsman also instructs the second whipper-in to keep to the high ground, telling him approximately in which direction he is drawing. The second whipper-in has met at this fixture earlier in the season, has been in the area during the cubhunting season, and therefore has quite a good idea of where to go.

ON POINT

You glance at your watch and notice that it is nearly ten minutes past eleven. Your pack meets at eleven, and you know that hounds always move off promptly at ten past the hour. You look up just in time to see the huntsman nod at his whippers-in. Both of them disappear toward the first draw so they can take up their positions well in advance of the hounds entering the covert, just in case a "seasoned" fox hears the horses on the road and leaves the covert before hounds enter.

Soon after, the huntsman leads the pack away from the meet in the same direction. He does not blow his horn on leaving the meet. Lord Daresbury used to say that blowing the horn on leaving the meet was "a terrible Cockney practice." Also, any fox lying in a covert close by will be gone on hearing it. You will also notice that the huntsman does not carry the horn between his top two buttons. The horn is in its correct place: in the case on his saddle. Some huntsmen have the habit of riding across the country with their hunting horn between their coat buttons—a very good way to break their ribs if they have a fall. The hunting horn, when not being used, should always be in its case when the huntsman is mounted.

As you stand at covertside, you are astonished to see a latecomer riding toward the covert from your right. Not only has he the bad manners to be late, but instead of joining the field, he rides up to the first whipper-in and starts talking to him. This has put the whipper-in in a difficult position. He knows that the huntsman expects him to be where he is, and he also knows that not only will he get a dressing-down from the huntsman if he is caught talking, but the fox could be headed. Nor does he want to be rude. Therefore he touches his cap to the member and says that he has to move further along the covertside. The whipper-in then rides away to re-position himself. The first whipper-in is not very comfortable with having to move, but he has tried to position himself in such away that he can see most of the area that he has left. It was lucky that the latecomer had not approached the second whipper-in, as being inexperienced he would most probably have taken up the conversation and, if caught by the hunts-man, received yet another blasting. Lord Daresbury would say if two people are seen standing aside in deep conversa-tion, it is generally accepted that at least one of them knows nothing about foxhunting!

Both whippers-in hear the huntsman turn back in the covert, and hold their positions. The first whipper-in hears the little birds chattering (Pat Meehan, one of the best whippers-in I had when hunting the County Limerick Foxhounds, always maintained that the little birds informed him when a fox was on its legs in covert), gets a brief glimpse of the fox as it comes out of the covert and slips back in again. He says nothing. He knows that the huntsman is sure there is a fox about or he would not have drawn back through the covert. He also knows that the huntsman does not like a lot of noise and that he likes his hounds to find their foxes themselves.

If the huntsman had finished drawing the covert, the whipper-in would have quietly told him what he had seen.

If two people are seen standing aside in deep conversation, it is generally
accepted that at least one of them knows nothing about foxhunting.

But for now he sits quietly and listens. He also hears Wagtail
whimper, and he checks his girth. His horse cocks its ears as
the pack opens on the line, but does not move.

You can just see the second whipper-in in the distance, sitting motionless on his horse. He has much to think about: Will
he be able to get a count of the hounds when they eventually
go away? The huntsman will want to know if the whole pack
is on. When they go away will they go in the direction of that
busy road, and what is his quickest way of getting to it? The
huntsman also told him about the farmer who does not want
the hunt, but he is not quite sure which farm he was talking
about. He is worried about all these things, because he knows
that if he gets it wrong he will get the rough edge of the huntsman's tongue. He is wondering at that moment whether he has
chosen the right career when he hears the pack open.

Meanwhile, the first whipper-in watches as the fox leaves the covert. It comes out almost at the same place where it had gone back in earlier. It pauses for a second and looks to its left. The whipper-in was once told by an experienced huntsman that when a fox looks in a certain direction when it exits a covert, that is the direction it will eventually make for even if it carries on straight. The whipper-in thinks about this, but keeps quiet until the fox is well away from the covert. He knows that if he holloas too soon the fox may well turn back into the covert. He has often seen this happen when a fox was over half a field away. He knows that Mr. Jorrocks was correct when he counted to twenty before holloaing "the old customer" away.

THE RUN

He holloas only once, and knows the huntsman has heard by the way he cheers his hounds. The hounds pour out of the covert, and he counts them as they race away on the line. They are all there. He is delighted that a first-season dog hound was first on the line throwing his tongue with a great voice. He must remember to tell the huntsman this. The huntsman comes out of the covert blowing the "gone away," and on hearing from the first whipper-in that all the hounds are on, he blows the *"cope forrard"* to instruct the second whipper-in to come on since no hounds have been left behind. This note on the horn sounds almost the way it is written. The second whipper-in has heard the signal from the huntsman, but he still keeps where he is on the high ground. He sees that the hounds are not heading for the busy road, which is a relief to him. Therefore, he tries to get some idea of where they may be heading. He remembers that when the hounds were last in this part of the country, he received a cursing because he had not been on the railway line that ran through it. Hounds are not running toward it, but they are running parallel with it. Therefore he canters on between the pack and the railway line, trying to keep to the high ground so he can see what is going on.

Some huntsmen like to have a whipper-in riding with them. This huntsman does not. If he cannot see his whippers-in, he is a happy man. He likes both of his whippers-in well on, either viewing the fox, seeking out information from people that may have viewed it, or using their heads to get on to a major road or railway.

You noticed the first whipper-in, when the hounds checked on the road, turn left to go up beside the road. You wondered what he was doing. He had seen that the hounds had approached the road, and knowing that half a mile up the road was a blind bend, he went straight to it. It may be a quiet road, but it only takes one car to cause an accident. He heard the pack open as they took the line from the road and he continues on downwind, knowing that they are running toward the small covert that always has a herd of deer in it.

He may have delayed on the road too long, and in his haste to get to the other side of the covert he jumps a rather large fence out of the plough into plough. His horse clears it well, but on landing its front legs sink into the plough, and it turns over. Fortunately both horse and rider rise up unscathed, but the whipper-in knows that he will not get to the covert before the hounds get there. He can only hope that the second whipper-in has had the good sense to get on.

Unfortunately, the second whipper-in has had his mind on the railway line, terrified of getting a cursing if hounds run toward it, and he is not at the covert. He, too, has dwelt too long and arrives at the covert just in time to see the pack going away, and one hound going out on the opposite side hunting a deer. He sets off in pursuit, and his heart drops

Now he can only hope that the second whipper-in has
had the good sense to get on forward.

when he sees which hound it is. Even the first whipper-in de-
tests this hound. However, because of its breeding, the huntsman wants it to have a chance.

It is a young hound, prone to riot, but that is not all of
the problem. It is usually easy to stop, but once stopped it

will not follow. Sure enough, having got it stopped, it is the same story. It will not follow the whipper-in. Almost in tears of frustration, he gets off his horse and removes the *couples* from his saddle. Several more precious minutes are lost as he tries to catch this hound. No easy thing when having to hold a horse at the same time. At last, after much cajoling, he gets the couples on the hound, and, tying the thong of his whip onto the second collar, he remounts and rides on in the direction he thinks the hounds have gone.

Luckily for him, the pack has checked on the plough, giving him time to catch up. As soon as he hears the hounds he jumps off his horse and releases the errant hound. It is as much as he can do to stop himself from giving the hound a cut of his whip to send it on its way, but he knows that you and the rest of the field are watching, as you stand with the Field Master waiting for the pack to get away from the plough.

The huntsman, believe it or not, is aware that this hound has been missing. At every opportunity he counts his hounds, and if any are missing he tries to think which ones they are. He got a count soon after the deer incident and realized that they were all there except for one—the one his first whipper-in has told him about on several occasions. He knows that a whipper-in sees a lot more of what certain hounds are doing than he does. He also knows that his first whipper-in has a brain and knows what he is talking about. He thinks that perhaps, breeding aside, this will be the young hound's last day with the pack. He will find it another home. Yet he is surprised to see the hound join the pack as they run into the rough fields.

The first whipper-in, on reaching the small covert that held the deer, is a little at a loss where hounds have gone. He knows that they were running downwind, but having the fall and then a little trouble catching his horse, he has got behind. Therefore, he makes for a piece of high ground where he pulls his horse up to survey the countryside. He listens, but hears nothing. Then far enough away on his left he sees a flock of sheep huddled in the corner of a field. Further, some cattle are running, and then he sees the mounted field standing by some ploughed fields. Guessing that hounds have checked on the plough and taking note that hounds had still been running with the wind, he rides on to once again get in front of the pack. You do not see the first whipper-in, as he does not come up from behind. He comes from the side, circumnavigating the plough, to get well downwind, knowing full well that there could be another fox in the rough fields beyond.

But you did see the second whipper-in release the hound and then ride away toward the right, searching for some high ground. The first whipper-in took up his position just in time to see the fresh fox come away. It is not always easy to tell a fresh fox from a hunted one, but to the experienced eye of the first whipper-in, there was no doubt the fox was clean. That does not necessarily mean a lot, but the fox was not over-hurried, and his body was well off the ground. The hunted fox may or may not be dirty, but his *brush* will be down and its back arched. If it is dead beat, its mouth will be closed. If it has its mouth open and tongue hanging out, there is still quite a lot left in the engine.

Lord Daresbury, when hunting the Belvoir Hounds in George Tongues' absence, told the story of viewing the hunted fox into a fence. The fox went through the fence at speed, but on reaching the other side it closed its mouth and walked. He then knew that the fox was his.

Stopping the hounds off the fresh fox was an easy maneuver this time for the first whipper-in. All he had to do was position himself on the fox's line and turn his horse's head toward the pack, shouting the words, "bike, go bike" while banging his whip on his saddle flap. The pack is downwind. Therefore not only will they hear the huntsman's horn as he blows for them, but they will also hear the three couples of hounds that have stayed with the hunted fox. This all makes the first whipper-in's job easier. He can make as much noise as he likes without the three couples hearing him. If the splinter group had run upwind, then his job would have been more difficult as he would have had to try and stop them quietly so as not to disturb the three couples that are running downwind. He would not have had the advantage of the pack hearing the huntsman's horn or the cry of the three couples that are hunting on.

This to you as a field member may all sound very easy, but trying to stop a high-mettled pack of hounds or a breakaway group of the same type on their legitimate quarry is not easy. On many occasions, to stop a breakaway group, the whipper-in may have to lie to them. He will get to their heads, stop them, and then gallop back the way they had come halloaing as if he had a fox in view. Once at the end of the day in Limerick, four couples of hounds were missing. It was late in the day, fog was coming in on the Kerry side of where we had been. The whipper-in was looking for the four couples that had gone high up into the Mullaghariek Forestry. There was difficulty in getting about, and vision was bad with the fog, but he came upon the hounds, which were still hunting. The whipper-in could not get to them, but when they checked, one hound came to him. Jumping off his horse he caught hold of the hound and twisted one of its ears until it called out in pain, and then he holloaed. The rest of the hounds came to him, and he quickly remounted and cantered away with them. Perhaps not quite an honest way of doing things, but he was able to return these hounds to his huntsman. He obviously did not tell his huntsman how he had managed it, nor would we condone this practice, but in this case it prevented four couples of hounds being left out all night and perhaps being killed on a road or railway line.

With the pack reunited, the first whipper-in again *sinks the wind* (goes on downwind) to try and get a view. Galloping over the open country and taking the fences in your stride, you and the rest of the field are able to keep the pack in sight. Then as the Field Master checks the field to stop them from getting too close to the pack, you see overhead, two fields in front of the hounds, six crows dipping. The huntsman has also seen them, and he knows that the crows are mobbing the fox.

This pleases the huntsman, but after a couple more fields the hounds check. Almost immediately, you see the second whipper-in ride up to the huntsman. There is a brief exchange. The huntsman calls for the hounds and gallops forward. The whipper-in quietly puts the pack onto him with the words, "get on to him, get on, on, on."

He knows the crows are mobbing the fox.

Now, the second whipper-in had not seen the fox. He had just missed it. But a farm worker had told him exactly where it had gone and how long it had been gone. He also told him that it "looked as though it had work done."

By going to the huntsman and telling him this, the second whipper-in was able not only to take the huntsman straight to where the farm worker had seen the fox, but was able to put the hounds on and also prevent the pack from taking the heel line. The second whipper-in had saved the huntsman precious minutes, and the pack is once again running with a good head toward the boundary wall of the large estate. Both whippers-in are aware that there is a river running through it. The second whipper-in has gone through the main gates, crossed the river via the bridge to wait in case the fox crosses the river by the bridge. Meanwhile the first whipper-in has got on beyond the property. The two of them know that the pack is now closing on the fox and they are both working closer together.

The first whipper-in, viewing the fox out of the wall and into the hedge, holloas. The second whipper-in quickly goes to the huntsman to push the hounds on to him. You will notice that there is now an excitement about the staff that you have not noticed before. There is excitement, but it is a controlled excitement—no noise, no fuss.

Now the second whipper-in moves to the end of the hedge. Perhaps the second whipper-in was wrong in doing this, as once the huntsman had reached the hedge, the first whipper-in was in control of the situation. The second whipper-in should have gone to the other side of the hedge, but as you stand watching, you realize that his horse has just about had enough. Once the first whipper-in sees that the huntsman knows where the fox entered the hedge he puts his horse at it, clears it well, and gallops down the hedge to stand opposite the second whipper-in.

· You see a hound flash out of the hedge past the second whipper-in, which distracts him. As he turns to watch the hound, the fox darts out between himself and the huntsman. Nothing is said, but the second whipper-in knows, as he tries to get his tired horse into a canter, that he will be getting a lecture from the huntsman when they have returned to the kennels. He will be blamed for letting the fox out of the hedge; he should have ignored the hound that flashed out. Every huntsman likes to reward his hounds after a good hunt, and his whippers-in are there to assist him in this aim. The second whipper-in should not have been distracted, but hopefully the huntsman will not be too hard on him and put it down to lack of experience.

The fox has shot his bolt, but why he did not go into the drain is anybody's guess. Perhaps it was occupied by a *vixen* with *cubs*.

TO GROUND

It is slow work now across the last couple of fields. The check short of the drain has given the fox an advantage and he just makes it to an earth in the covert. The huntsman dismounts, gives his horse to a foot follower, and goes into the covert to cheer his hounds. He is soon joined by the first whipper-in. You notice the second whipper-in has not moved from his position. He is waiting to see if a fresh fox goes, which would enable the huntsman to continue on. In his heart he is praying that this does not happen as he knows that his horse has had enough. Like most young people, he has not yet learned how to save his horse. This time his prayer is answered. He hears the huntsman calling the pack away from the earth, but he continues waiting until the huntsman and first whipper-in are remounted. Then he rides over to join them.

You are standing close enough to hear the first whipper-in say, "All on, sir," as they ride away from the covert before the second whipper-in joins them. When he arrives you also hear the huntsman ask him how many hounds he has. You watch the second whipper-in as he tries to count them and hear him reply that there is one missing. "Count them again," demands the huntsman. After a couple of minutes you hear the second whipper-in say, "All on, sir." The huntsman says nothing. Much to the second whipper-in's relief, you hear the Master giving the huntsman the order for home.

Normally the huntsman would not blow the long mournful notes of "going home" on his horn, just in case the pack picked up the line of a fox as they are hacking back to the hound van. But today is the last day of the season, and also most of the horses have had enough. You listen to those long notes and wonder where the huntsman gets all the wind from his lungs for such long, lingering, delightful notes.

THE EDUCATION OF A WHIPPER-IN

Your thoughts go back to the day's hunting and in particular to the first whipper-in. This has been his last day with your hunt, and you will miss him, as will many others of the mounted field. He has done much to help your huntsman show good sport for the last three seasons. There have been many hunts when his skill and woodcraft have helped the huntsman when all appeared to be lost. He had the knack of being in the right place at the right moment. You remember hounds checking in a herd of cattle in the same place they had lost the fox the previous meet, but this time the first whipper-in was well on and viewed the fox out of the cattle, enabling the huntsman to get his hounds on quickly through those large pastures.

He was an artist in seeing a fox away from the two huge forestries that you have in your country. He did not gallop about the outside when the hounds were running inside the forestry. He stationed himself on the high ground on the downwind side and waited patiently. He only holloaed the fox away when hounds were not running. If the pack was running and he viewed a fox away, he would slip quickly into the covert and tell the huntsman what he had seen. If the huntsman decided that the fox was going in the direction he favored, they would wait their moment. You have seen the huntsman catch hold of his hounds when they came onto a ride and, with the help of his whipper-in, gallop out to where the fox had been viewed. What good hunts you have enjoyed from these large strongholds, thanks to the first whipper-in.

There was no doubt that this whipper-in and the huntsman worked hand in glove. They rarely spoke to each other, but were definitely on the same wavelength. At times you had the impression that they were working by telepathy.

You were much surprised at the start of a good hunt in mid-season, when the pack had divided, to see the huntsman stop his lot and take them onto those that were with the first whipper-in. At the end of the day, when horses and hounds were loaded up, you asked the huntsman why he had done this. The huntsman explained that he was in a better position to stop his lot than the first whipper-in was with his. It had nothing to do with which way the fox was going; it was just a matter of getting the pack reunited as quickly as possible. Then there were those days when the first whipper-in hunted hounds in the huntsman's absence. It was a delight to watch him. He never interfered with them; he left them alone. When congratulated on a good hunt, he just replied that he was lucky to be allowed to hunt such a wonderful pack of hounds that had been bred and hunted by such a great huntsman. A class act to the final day.

With these thoughts your mind turns to the second whipper-in, a new boy with enthusiasm bubbling out of him. He was indeed lucky to be starting his career with your hunt and to be serving under one of the best huntsmen in the world. He only has one horse a day, while the huntsman and first whipper-in have two, but his horses are good. Your Master knows it costs just as much to feed a bad horse as it does a good one. He has also told you that mounting hunt staff badly should be a criminal offense! They have a job to do, and they cannot do it if badly mounted, nor should they be asked to do so.

The second whipper-in, as you know, has only one horse, not necessarily as a saving to the hunt, but to teach him to save his horse by staying on the high ground and not jumping fences for fun. You have felt sorry for him on occasion. Many times he has had a cursing from the huntsman. Several times you have seen him learning from his mistakes. There was that horrible wet day in November when he had counted hounds and reported to the huntsman that one was missing. The huntsman told him to go back and find it. You had earlier heard the first whipper-in tell the huntsman that they were all on. The second whipper-in did as he was told and it was not until the end of the day when the pack was safely in the hound van that he returned drowned to the skin, but did not flinch when he was told by the huntsman in your hearing that it had never been missing. You may think that too much emphasis is made about the second whipper-in counting hounds, but it is essential that he learns to do this, not only to let the huntsman know how many hounds he has, but also so the huntsman will know approximately the area where a hound has gone missing. Therefore, if it is still missing at the end of the day he will know where to look for it.

The hunt staff must learn discipline. We do not want the whipper-in who, when asked by his huntsman during a check in a good hunt how many hounds they had, replied, "Enough to be going on with, sir." Nor do we want the whipper-in who jumped into the middle of the pack as the huntsman was putting them into covert to draw for a fox. "What the hell do you think you are doing?" demanded the huntsman. "Just trying to scatter them about for you!" replied the whipper-in.

What a good hunt they had from the "Cat and Fiddle." You had lost a shoe and were riding on the grass beside the road back to the trailer when you heard hounds running toward you. You pulled up to watch, just as the second whipper-in came up behind you and went on a few yards up the road and stopped. You saw the fox come onto the road in front of him, turn up the road, and continue on out of sight. You saw the hounds come at pace onto the road; their cry ceased and the pack milled about trying to regain the line. The huntsman arrived with the field hard on his heels. You saw the second whipper-in telling the huntsman what he had seen, and you also saw the huntsman give him such a blasting that he was almost reduced to tears.

In this case the fox may have continued along this quiet country road for miles. The huntsman would have no idea how far it had gone and even his "road running" hounds may have difficulty taking the line, especially if a car came down the fox's line. You realized the whipper-in should have gone after the fox and put him off the road or seen where it left the road. Another lesson learned for the second whipper-in, even if it was the hard way!

Yet, you remember other occasions when he had got it right, although it drew no praise from the huntsman. You first realized his potential when hounds divided during a morning's cubhunting. Hounds were hunting in the big woods, and you saw the two couples go away. You also saw the second whipper-in set off in pursuit of them. That morning you had a business meeting and had to leave the field early. As you rode toward home, you heard the second whipper-in coming toward you. He was calling hounds in a musical voice, "Come along, cope, cope, cope, cope, come along, cope." As he appeared you saw that he had a couple and a half with him, and, just as he took off his cap saying, "Good night, sir," the fourth hound came

He was calling hounds in a musical voice.

galloping up to him. What a difference, you thought, to one of his predecessors who came back to the huntsman saying that he had stopped the renegades, but when he had them stopped they would not follow him. He had not lasted the season.

Then there was that frightening incident in the middle of the season, when hounds were hunting in the "not so fashionable" part of the country. It is a difficult part of the country to get about, with a very busy highway on the edge of it. It was toward this highway that hounds were running unaccompanied, huntsman and field having been held up by a wire fence. It was quite some achievement on the second whipper-in's part not only to have reached the road, but also to have stopped the pack from getting on it.

Just last week, you saw hounds running toward a stick heap, and you thought to yourself, "That is the finish of the hunt; the fox always gets into it." Happily, you were wrong. The second whipper-in had got forward and turned the fox away as it approached.

The one thing that does strike your mind is the fact that when out hunting with your home pack, you never hear a whip being cracked. If the whippers-in are stopping hounds or turning a fox away from an open earth or stick heap, you notice that they do this by getting to the hounds' heads and slapping their saddle flaps with the whip and using their voices.

There is to your mind one thing that is certain: the second whipper-in is showing initiative. You just hope that the huntsman is not so hard on him that he kills it. But again, you think of how many second whippers-in have served under him and gone on to better themselves.

Your mind now turns to next season. You must spare a sympathetic thought for the huntsman, as he will then have a new first whipper-in who does not know his ways or the country. He will also still have an inexperienced second whipper-in. Let us hope that at least he will have a good scenting season!

FOUR

WHAT IS THE FIELD MASTER DOING?

When Far Behind Him in the Vale
Strings out the Beaten Hunt,
With easy Grace, He keeps his Place,
His Rightful Place in Front.

—Will H. Ogilvie

Very few people that hunt are aware of the huge role the Field Master plays during the course of a hunting day. It is to him that you bid "Good morning," after having paid your respects to the Master and hunt staff.

Lord Daresbury, when Master of the Belvoir (UK), always wore a top hat and swallow tails. On being asked how people recognized him as the Master and Field Master dressed in such a way, his answer was, "If a person does not know who I am, they should not be hunting with me."

The Field Master may be a Master of the hunt, or he or she may be appointed to the position by the Master. In either case, the position is a demanding one. It requires exceptional knowledge of the hunting country and how to get through it when hounds are running, whether by gate or panel. The Field Master must be well mounted on a bold horse, for he has no

On being asked how people recognized him as the Master and
Field Master dressed in such a way, Lord Daresbury's answer was,
"If a person does not know who I am, they should not be hunting with me."

one to follow. The Field Master must also possess a delicate
balance of diplomacy and discipline. His ever-present conflict
is the contradiction of giving field members pleasure of their
hunting day with a front row seat to the action, while at the
same time controlling them in their exuberance so as not to
interfere with huntsman and hounds. The great Field Masters
also have an innate sense of venery, which keeps them in tune
with the huntsman and guides their positioning of the field.

We will assume you know your Field Master and have ex-
tended the proper greeting. It is the last day of the season,
and there are quite a number of mounted visitors from neighboring packs. You may notice that the Master has spent more
time than usual in conversation with the Field Master. There
is a large mounted field in attendance, but some of the coun-

try has already been harrowed and rolled. For the Master it has been quite a trouble-free season, and he or she wants nothing to go wrong on this, the last day, to spoil it. The Master also informs the Field Master of the late-night call he had received from the farmer who does not want the hunt on his land today.

This is not a huge problem to the Field Master as he knows the country like the back of his hand. His brain is already working on how to avoid this property if hounds run close to it. The Master also talks to him about the order of coverts to be drawn, although the Field Master has already noted the direction of the wind and guessed correctly how the huntsman would draw the selected country.

When the Field Master has finished his conversation with the Master, you see him turn to talk with the huntsman. He asks the huntsman if he requires a couple of experienced field members to go on point duty. The huntsman thinks it may be a good idea to send two onto certain parts of the first covert, as it is quite large and his whippers-in will not be able to view all of the out-side area.

There are times when the Field Master may send a reliable person on to keep the huntsman in sight. This person acts as a go-between if the huntsman does not want to make a lot of noise. The go-between can report back to the Field Master as to what is going on, and the Field Master, always concerned about getting left behind, need not crowd the huntsman, especially in covert, with his large field. This is also a great help when the huntsman is making a cast and requires plenty of room.

If the Field Master is a long way from the hounds he will look to see which way the whippers-in have their horses' heads pointed. A whipper-in always has his horse pointed toward the hounds. That knowledge can be of great help to the Field Master if he has temporarily lost contact with the pack.

If hounds are out of sight, the Field Master will look to see which way
the whipper-in's horse's head is pointing.

Having spoken to the Master and huntsman, the Field
Master now calls for the attention of the mounted field. He asks
them to please keep to the headlands of any rolled or seeded
fields. He also informs them that there is one farm on which nobody must set foot. He names the farm and the landowner, and
he explains the reason why nobody is to cross it today.

POSITIONING HIS FIELD

When the Master gives the huntsman the order to move off,
you wait with the Field Master and the rest of the mounted
field to give the huntsman and hounds a little distance before
following them to the first draw. On the way you see a hound
stop to empty itself. The Field Master also sees it. He pulls his

horse up and raises his hand, bringing the field to a halt. Once the hound has finished and caught up with the pack, the Field Master continues on. He, like the huntsman and whippers-in, has much on his mind. He knows that a bad decision on his part can not only ruin a hunt for the field, but can also make life very difficult for the huntsman and hounds. The huntsman, being a professional, does not have the safety valve that an amateur huntsman has: the freedom to blast the Field Master if his hounds are overridden or jumped on! Even so, the Field Master may get one of those withering looks that only a fired-up professional huntsman can give.

On reaching the covert, the Field Master calls for a halt as the huntsman goes through the wicket gate with his hounds to start drawing. As you look about, you realize that the Field Master is holding the field on some high ground where you have a good view of the surrounding country. You may notice also that, as the huntsman is drawing into the wind, you on the downwind side can easily hear him.

You see the latecomer ride toward you as the first whipper-in leaves his position. As he gets closer you see the Field Master beckon him. You do not hear what the Field Master is saying, but you can tell by the look on the latecomer's face that it is not flattery. When the Field Master has finished the latecomer makes his way meekly to the back of the field.

The covert being drawn is a large but not a huge covert. If it were much larger, the Field Master would have given the huntsman a little grace and then followed him through the wicket gate. The Field Master is not keen on taking the field into coverts no matter how big they are, as he knows that by doing so he is foiling the rides. Therefore if he has to go into a covert, he tries to keep to one ride only. He does not gallop about after the huntsman when hounds have found, but tries to hold his field in the center of the covert. He may also send on with the huntsman an experienced member of the field who can be trusted to report back. Foxes will often run a ride for long distances. The Field Master knows this and that is why he tries to keep to one ride. All the others will be clean for the hounds to hunt over and along without checking due to the foil of sweaty horses.

Perhaps when standing inside a large covert the Field Master may see a fox cross the ride in front of him, and if hounds are not speaking he stands with his field and sends another field member to where the fox was seen. The field member holloas, *"tally ho over,"* pointing his horse's head and hunting cap in the direction the fox has gone. You have noticed in the past that the Field Master never leaves his field unattended.

THE RUN

The Field Master hears the long notes of the "gone away," being on the high ground and also on the downwind side. You can see the pack going away like a flock of pigeons with a great cry, and you can feel the tension of the other members of the field. Then all is excitement as the Field Master sets off in pursuit of the flying pack. The Field Master is a good horseman and a born leader. He leads from the front, knowing it is a waste of time shouting at people's backs. The only way to control a field of hard-riding horseman is to be able to turn and face them. He, like the huntsman, does not ride for reputation. He does not over-face his horse at his fences. He knows his country and the location of all hunt fences. He is also aware that on occasion it is better to take the field through a gate rather than knock a tricky landowner's fences about.

A persistent worry to the Field Master when using gates is the chance of a gate being left open and livestock either getting out onto the road or getting mixed up with livestock in an adjoining field. The hunt may or may not have gate shutters, but you have noticed that when using a gate the Field Master often asks a reliable person to stay back and make sure it is closed. This is a hard thing to expect somebody to do in a good hunt, but as you know full well, it is this type of benevolent sportsman-landowner that helps keep fox-hunting alive and hunting country open. This may appear to you rather unnecessary if there are gate shutters following on behind, but the Field Master is aware that the gate shutters may have stayed back to make some temporary repairs to a fence or retrieve some livestock that may have got out.

You have to admire the way that the Field Master crosses the country, giving you and the other field members every opportunity to see what the hounds are doing. If you have talked to your Field Master, you know that he is acutely aware that he is responsible for giving everybody in the field the chance to enjoy every moment of the day without hindering the huntsman or the hounds.

The Field Master is not only watching the huntsman, he is also watching the hounds. Like the huntsman, he is also anticipating hounds checking. It is not an easy position being a Field Master, and he requires all the assistance he can get from his field. His authority must never be questioned.

As hounds reach the road, the Field Master, suspecting that hounds may check, has slowed down. He brings his field to a halt on some high ground half a field away. He is aware that hounds have been running downwind, and is also aware that the rising sweat from the horses will drift downwind. There is not a lot that he can do about this except keep his field quiet and their horses still. The sweat from the horses may drift down with the wind, but as he holds his field a little to the right of the pack and the fox has turned left to run up the road, no harm has been done.

Soon you are again galloping on with the Field Master. Notice that he takes the shortest route to keep with hounds, but does not jump anything extraordinary to keep up. As you gallop with him, you can see he is always looking a field ahead for the next jumping place. You may have noticed also that when he jumped the two brooks, he did so each time beside a tree. If you were to ask him later why he did this, he would point out that the roots from the tree hold the bank together, giving the horse more grip on the take-off. This practice also lessens the erosion caused by numerous horses climbing the bank. Crossing the bank country in Limerick, we always tried to pick a place beside a strong bush or tree for the same reasons.

Now his pace slows as he sees the deer leave the small covert. The Field Master is aware that the pack will not riot on the deer, but he also knows that the foil of the deer will check the pack or slow it down. He does not want to make matters worse by getting too close, either pushing hounds over the line or making the foil worse with the horses. You do not think this was a serious check, as hounds are soon running hard, and once again the Field Master puts on the pace. But very soon he has to slow the field when the pack enters the farm of arable land. As hounds are brought to their noses, the Field Master takes note of the wind. The pack has been running slightly across the wind since it left the road. Therefore, as the huntsman casts his hounds over the plough, the Field Master walks with his field along a headland, making sure that once again the sweat from the horses does not drift into or beyond the pack.

Notice that, at this check, the Field Master consciously keeps walking forward. Why? If he does not and the pack goes away fast, the field will have to gallop through the deep plough to catch up, thereby sapping the strength of the horses.

The next real check occurs as the hounds reach the river. There the Field Master holds you well back at the top of the field that sweeps down to the river. He has done this not only to give the mounted field the chance to see what the hounds are doing, but also to give the huntsman plenty of room to cast his hounds.

The Field Master is also aware that the fox is not far in front of the pack. He also saw the crows dipping. He knows that crows will often dip to mob a hunted fox, as will magpies, and he also knows that once the hounds have left the demesne and reached the hedgerow, it will be slow work for the mounted field. You have all had a good gallop; several horses have nearly had enough; but now is not the time to press the pack or foil the line. It is now that you will appreciate that this pack can not only run sharply and accurately, but they can also hunt and work for their line. The Field Master is still moving forward, trying to give his field every opportunity to see the closing stages of this good hunt.

Hounds and huntsman have provided good sport. Now, nothing must interfere to prevent them from accounting for their fox. No huntsman wants to enter into his hunting diary, as Mr. Jorrocks often did, "Accounted for him by losing him."

DAMAGE REPORTS AND OTHER RESPONSIBILITIES

As the huntsman dismounts to go into the covert where hounds are marking, you notice that the Field Master also dismounts, turns his horse to face the wind, and loosens its girth. This obviously helps the horse to get its wind back, even though the pace has been slow over the last few fields.

The hunt may be over for you and the rest of the field, but the day has not finished for the Field Master. As he stands with his horse, several members of the field approach to inform him of the damage to fences that he may not be aware of. This pleases the Field Master, as he and the Master can tackle these problems swiftly before the landowners complain. The Field Master is also relieved that hounds and horses did not go near the farmer who, on this occasion, did not want the hunt. Therefore the hunt will be welcome next season.

Naturally after such a good hunt there is talk and laughter, but as the huntsman reappears with his hounds, the Field Master remounts and puts himself once again between his field and the pack. He always wants to make certain that you and the other riders have their horses' heads pointed toward the hounds. It has been known for even a tired horse to kick a hound.

As the Master rides up to join his huntsman, you notice that the Field Master again gives the hounds a little grace before following on. Once again you reflect on the day's hunting. You recall that when the Field Master jumped onto a road, he presented his horse at an angle to the fence, giving him more of a chance to land on the grass verge. Also, once on the road, he made his horse stand until the next rider landed. This helped to prevent the next rider's horse from turning sharply on the road and perhaps slipping and falling. You also noticed when he jumped a dry wall that he made his horse buck over it by jumping it from a standstill and making his horse use his hocks. When you questioned him about this, he explained that with all the loose stones on the landing side, a horse has more of a chance of staying on its feet if it lands on them slowly. If the horse lands on them at speed and the stones roll or the horse slips on one, it often results in a fall.

As with everything else in the hunting field there are exceptions. I remember, during a hunt in the Limerick Wall Country, putting on a little pace going into a wall that was part of a derelict building. It was as well, because on the landing side a telegraph pole had been laid across parallel with the wall to make a place to fodder cattle. My father-in-law, Mr. A.R. Tarry, who was Field Master at the time, sensibly made his horse buck over. However, the horse's front legs landed between the wall and the telegraph pole, and they both turned over. Luckily, neither horse nor rider was hurt, and they continued on, although my father-in-law's hunting cap was badly damaged.

You were amused when you heard a young *thruster* ask the Field Master why he did not swim the river that ran through the estate. The answer was obvious: the bridge was close by. If the bridge had not been near, and the Field Master had not seen the huntsman cross, he would have asked what Captain Ronnie Wallace often referred to as "a lad of no consequence" to go into the river first while he held the field back. Your Field Master knows that anybody can get into the river, but it is sometimes difficult to get out.

Several horses in a river at the same time with no way out can be very dangerous. I have seen this happen several times. Once, my wife, Caroline, fell victim to these circumstances. Horses panicked, riders panicked, and she was knocked off midstream. Luckily she was not hurt and got to dry land safely, but because her horse got out on the opposite bank, her day was over.

Assuming the chosen field member comes out safely on the opposite bank, the Field Master would then ask the field to take their time. He would put his horse into the river a little above where the field member got out. Turning his horse's head slightly upstream, he would let the current take his swimming horse down to where his pilot got out.

You recall the Field Master of the neighboring pack that you hunted with a couple of times this season. He had a short temper and was forever shouting at the field or an individual member of the field, often using parade ground language. He fancied himself a good horseman and was convinced he was good at his job, but he was not. He jumped fences for the sake of jumping, often larking about while the huntsman was drawing for a fox. Consequently his horse was tired when hounds started to run, and he could not hold his place in front of the field. This made his temper worse, which took the pleasure out of the day's hunting for everybody. Feeling defensive, he would come up at a check and abuse those few mounted field members that had gone on without him, and were standing with their huntsman and hounds when he finally arrived.

As usual, during the hunt today there were a couple of occasions when one or two members of the field had pressed hounds a little, but the Field Master only had to turn in his saddle and quietly caution them. He knows that the mounted field members are there to enjoy themselves, and that the younger members would be a sorry lot if they did not have a certain amount of drive.

You will recall that he did not make a scene at the start of the day when the latecomer rode up to the whipper-in. Nor did many in the field notice him admonish a young man for riding wide on a field of seeds when he should have been close to the headland. The Field Master is a man of tact, and the mounted field respects him. He kept you in touch with hounds, yet he used your horses with economy. The respect of his field is obvious to you as, on approaching the trailers, each member thanks him for the day along with the Master and huntsman.

Even at this time of the day the Field Master is still in control. He asks the field to stand until the hunt staff have loaded the hounds safely into their trailer. He knows that flighty young hounds like to run around people, and by quietly waiting with the field, he once again reduces the chance of a hound being kicked.

During the day you noticed how well the Field Master for the second flight always seemed to have those people in the

The Field Master had only to turn in his saddle and quietly caution them.

correct place, giving them every opportunity to see what was going on either by keeping to the high ground or getting them forward quickly along a lane or road, but never in any way interfering with the progress of the hounds. He had them close enough to see, but far enough away not to interfere.

FIVE

WHAT ARE THE HOUNDS DOING?

The bitch from the Belvoir, the dog from the
   Quorn,
The pick of the litter our Puppy was born,
And the day he was entered he flew to the horn,
But rating and whipcord he treated with scorn.

—C. T. Whyte Melville

Your horse has been looked after and is well tucked up for the night. You have enjoyed a long, hot soak in the tub, perhaps with a glass of your favorite beverage. Now sitting beside the fire in a comfortable chair with a second drink, you think of the season that has just ended and what you have learned about the hounds. The hunt today was a good hunt, but you enjoyed it especially because you have been taking an increasing interest in the hounds and what they are doing.

At the meet you eventually counted the hounds correctly. You know you got it right because you overheard the huntsman telling the Master how many he had out. During the day you tried to count them whenever you got the chance, and you realized that it was not an easy thing to do, even when they were at a check.

Although you could not see the hounds in the first covert, you could hear them and you tried to tell what they were doing by listening to the cry. You are quite pleased with yourself as you read the cry correctly and understood what was happening from the time Wagtail whimpered.

When the hounds left the covert, you noticed they were packed up well together—a blanket could cover them. You had placed yourself as close to the Field Master as possible and were in a position to see the hounds as they ran in front. You noted and admired the way they swung as one, where the fox had turned down a fence, not one hound going beyond the line, therefore not wasting a second. It is when hounds flash over the line or run on jealously without the scent that the fox is given an advantage.

You admired the way the pack swung as one,
where the fox had turned, not wasting a second.

CHECKS

When hounds slowed down on what looked like a normal field, you wondered why. The cry had also diminished and the pack was a little strung out. You could see nothing that could have foiled the scent: there was no livestock in the field; there was no smoke drifting with the wind, or exhaust fumes. Looking down at the ground you noticed grey granules in the grass: artificial manure. It had not caused a serious check, but it had slowed hounds down.

When artificial fertilizer was first introduced to Ireland it proved to be a nuisance to the Limerick hounds. When the pack reached a single field dressed with artificial, it would drive on across the field, pick up the line on the other side, and run on with a great cry. All very well until reaching two or three fields in a row that had fertilizer on them. Crossing them, the pack would gradually slow down. Once the pack had stopped, I would go to them and cast back. If that failed, I would make a long cast forward.

Later on, your pack checked once again in a field. This time the reason for the check was obvious, as this field had been treated with natural manure. You watched as the pack tried to pick up the line forward. They failed, and, when turning back, fanned out trying every inch of the headlands. You noticed that even though the hounds had their heads down, they were still watching each other. You saw a dark hound stop and almost open; several hounds seeing this rushed to him, one whimpered but then silence. This gave the huntsman a clue as to what had caused the check. It was not only the manure, but also the fox had been headed. The huntsman had seen a tractor and trailer disappearing into the distance, and when he saw the dark hound turn back toward him he was pretty confident as to what had happened. Therefore he edged his hounds a little faster in the direction that the hound was pointing when it whimpered. A good move. The pack opened a little to the right of where it entered the field.

You think of the check on the road and you are pleased that one of the hounds that you picked out at the meet was the one that took the line of the fox up the road. You are not sure whether you picked this hound out because of his distinctive coloring or because you have seen him doing good things in the past. You are pretty certain it was this hound that took the line along the top of a stone wall during a nice hunt a couple of weeks ago.

RIOT

At the time you did not think the check among the deer was a very serious as it was over with quickly, but now as you sit thinking you realize how the hunt would have been ruined if the hounds had rioted on the deer. You have often smelled the scent of deer and know it is quite strong. You marvel that the hounds could take the line of the fox through the deer foil, but you saw them do it. This has got you thinking even more, and you start to understand that there is a lot more to foxhunting than jumping fences.

You saw the young hounds speak and then stop. You also saw the old hound go to them along with a couple of other hounds. The old hound stopped with its nose hard to the ground, then its stern started to move a little, it took a couple of paces forward and then it opened with a good note, at the same time sprinting away. With this, the rest of the pack joined in and were once again running well. This you thought was very impressive. You had seen hounds check in domestic stock many times, but this time it was a herd of deer running with the fox or at least on the fox's line. Hounds had every opportunity to riot, but they did not.

Hounds had every opportunity to riot, but they did not.

Major Field Marsham, who hunted the Bicester hounds and later the Eridge, maintained that the worst crime a pack of hounds could commit was changing from their quarry onto riot.

In America it is a great challenge to have a pack of hounds that is one hundred percent deer proof. Every country in the States has a certain number of white-tailed deer, but it must not be forgotten that in England most hunting countries have some type of deer, perhaps red deer, roe deer or the little munjac. Many of these were escapees from deer farms or open zoos. I remember Bill Lander and myself having to be very careful not to holloa a munjac in the Heythrop country when whipping-in to Captain Wallace. In the heat of the moment they could be mistaken for a bobtailed fox.

American huntsmen use many methods to teach their hounds not to riot on deer. The problem is more difficult for the American huntsman than the English huntsman. In England, where foxes are classed as vermin because of their excessive population, hounds experience more kills and know with greater certitude exactly what they should be hunting. That said, it must not be forgotten that those packs that hunt in the hill countries of England have to be very steady of riot when hunting through the many sheep. Often a sheep will jump up in front of the pack when least expected, and, living off the heather, they too smell very gamey. Therefore you will understand that hounds in any hunting country have to be riot free. However, I have not yet found a way to prevent the Rolling Rock hounds from hunting bear!

The check on the plough now comes to your mind. This baffled you a little as to why hounds checked, as on previous occasions you have seen hounds run well over ploughed land with the dust rising up behind them. Perhaps the answer may be that this plough was quite wet due to the previous day's rain, and the mud had stuck to the fox's feet, therefore helping to dull the scent. It was slow work across the plough. Every hound was trying, and occasionally the odd hound would open, but they could not put on the pressure. As you watched you noticed it was not always the same hound that opened: once it was a tricolored hound, then a dark dog hound, then a blue mottled bitch. Individually they were working, but as a pack they could not get going together until they reached the rough fields.

This hound work reminded you of a day earlier in the season. The meet had been held in the hill country, which consisted of many miles of open moorland. You watched as the huntsman drew some gorses blank, but as hounds came out of it one old hound opened. The rest of the pack joined him, and then you saw them steadily working the line in the same manner as the hounds had worked on the plough today.

It was again slow hound work. The huntsman kept well back, but when hounds hesitated you noticed that he nudged them on slightly in the direction that the lead hounds were leaning to. He was quiet doing this, but each time he was proven correct, as a hound would open. This slow work lasted for nearly twenty minutes, and then as hounds reached a small bunch of briars beside a wall they opened with a roar. You saw the fox top the wall and there followed a good hunt at top pace. At the end of the day you questioned the huntsman as to why the hounds hunted so slowly at the start. He explained that for that first twenty minutes the hounds were hunting the drag of the fox where it had been walking about in the night. The pack had un-kenneled it where it had lain down for the day.

Autumn hunting on the hills in Limerick provided many instances of this. One morning comes to mind on Ballingarry Hill. Hounds had hunted a fox to ground and were waiting to be rewarded. A unentered hound called Slasher wandered away from the pack. I watched him, telling my whipper-in to leave him alone. He had gone nearly a hundred yards when he opened. I left the terrier man to finish his work and took the pack on to Slasher. The pack took the drag for nearly thirty minutes before getting up to their fox and enjoying a good hill hunt.

During the 2003–2004 season the Keswick hounds with their huntsman, Tony Gammell, came to hunt the Rolling Rock country in Pennsylvania. It was a joy to see this pack of American hounds during the first draw of the day working the line of a fox that had been walking about and eventually getting up to it. Again a good hunt was enjoyed and the fox accounted for. The admirer of the American foxhound will enthuse that this type of hound has a better nose than most other breeds of hounds.

This could well be true, as a foxhound in America has to hunt much of the time under very dry conditions. Then later in the year it will be hunting over ice and snow. There is no doubt that the American foxhound and the Penn-Marydel also have great voices.

Hunting what is thought to be the drag of a fox in America can sometimes come to an abrupt end when the wild turkey eventually takes to its wings! Chris Howells, ex-huntsman of the Blue Ridge Hunt in Virginia, always claimed that he couldn't tell the difference in the cry of his hounds whether they were on fox or turkey!

He couldn't tell the difference in the cry of his hounds
whether they were on fox or turkey.

CHANGING FOXES

There is indeed much to think about when it comes to riot, but now your thoughts turn to the fresh fox that jumped up in the rough fields. You saw the fresh fox and you are now wondering how many times this happens during a day's hunting, or perhaps how often during the season. Obviously it happens more than the average member of the field realizes. A hunted fox will always try to pass the baton, either by running into a large covert where he knows there will be other foxes, or by rousing another fox out of a fence or a rough piece of land, as you saw today.

You remember the good hunt during the first week of January when hounds found a dog fox that was lying in a fence close to the first covert to be drawn. The pack settled straight away, skirting the covert to run straight across a good line of country for four miles when they entered a small covert. Hounds hardly appeared to delay in the covert before they were once more out in the open, with the "holloa" of a car follower ringing in your ears as he viewed the fox away. The huntsman had doubts, however. The pack was not running in the same style as it had before entering the covert. Several of his lead hounds had dropped back, and it appeared that scent was not as good as it had been. This could be true if the hunted fox was failing, but then the lead hounds would not have dropped back. Also, when the car follower holloaed, the huntsman judged that the fox should not have been in the position it was if it were the hunted one. There was nothing the huntsman could do with a large mounted field behind him and a good country in front of him. He continued on, but, sadly, because of the change, he did not account for his fox and had to stop the pack due to failing light.

Why not breed a pack of hounds that will not change foxes, you may wonder. There are times when it is necessary for a huntsman to change foxes. Perhaps there has been enough done in a certain area, as hounds have run all about locally when a fresh fox is viewed going away from the foil. The huntsman will catch hold of his hounds and take them onto the fresh fox. It will most probably take the pack a little time to get tuned in before it is away into clean country.

Perhaps if hounds run into a large wood they will rouse several foxes and the pack will divide. Under these circumstances the huntsman will let his hounds alone and wait for them to come up together for themselves. It is anybody's guess that they are on the hunted one unless it is viewed away. Lord Daresbury was once told that he had not gone away on the hunted fox. His reply was, "It is now."

Just after the rough fields you noticed the pack was running well and carrying a good head except for a couple of hounds that could not quite go the pace. One of them, you noticed, was a hound that had done a lot to keep the pack going over the plough and you had also noticed him doing well over the field that had been manured. The other one you were not quite sure about. It was a bitch, and when the day was over you described the hounds to the huntsman and inquired about them.

The huntsman explained to you that the hound that had worked so well over the foiled ground was an old stallion hound. He was in his last season, but would still do a couple of mornings' autumn hunting next season before being retired. It pleased the huntsman that the bitch could not keep up toward the end of the hunt, as it confirmed his suspicions that she was *in whelp*. He values her as a brood bitch and hopes she will produce a litter of whelps as good as she and the sire.

FOX SENSE

Every huntsman knows that he must breed for longevity, so that he has a pack of hounds like the old stallion hound. They are correct in make and shape so that they wear well and can hunt on into old age. Their fox sense and experience are invaluable to the pack and to the huntsman. When thinking of this, you think of the agility of the hounds as they scaled the demesne wall. It impressed you then and it impresses you now. The whole pack scaled the wall like cats. It was a sight you will find hard to forget. Only the brood bitch and the old stallion hound did not make it. They followed the huntsman through the gates before rejoining the pack at the river.

Now thinking about it in the calm of the evening, you realize that it was the old stallion hound who was winding the lily pads. He was also the first hound to throw his tongue in the river. You just hope that you will be able to see him hunt again before he is retired. The most exciting part of the hunt to your mind was when the fox was in the hedge with the hounds all around it. If the second whipper-in had not turned to watch the hound that had flashed out of the hedge he would have seen the fox coming and moved his horse, enabling hounds to catch their quarry. All huntsman like their hounds to be rewarded, and it is part of the whipper-in's job to assist him and the hounds to this aim.

In Captain Ronnie Wallace's *Manual of Foxhunting*, edited by Michael Clayton, the captain tells the story of his whipper-in (me!) viewing a fox in a field of brussels sprouts where it had clapped after a very good hunt. The captain came up quite excited asking, "Where is it? Where is it?" I made the fatal mistake of turning to answer his question, and while I did this the fox got up and disappeared. The hounds could not take the line of his failing scent in the stink of the sprouts. I was wrong for taking my eyes off it, but if I had not turned to answer the captain he would have given me a blasting for not looking at him when I was speaking to him! Only one winner there, and that was the fox.

It was slow hunting after the fox left the hedge, but you noticed that the hounds hunted well up together until they reached the earth. And you were impressed by the depth of their voices as they marked their fox to ground.

HOUND TYPES

You have heard quite a lot of talk at dinner parties about various types of hounds and their attributes. It is an endless discussion with so many theories and prejudices, but you must remember, it does not matter greatly which type of hound makes up a pack; eighty percent of the results depend on the handling of that pack.

Some people will say that hounds should be bred to suit the country that they hunt over. In some cases this could be true, such as the Fell packs that hunt over the rugged rocks and hills of the Lake District. Another example would be the College Valley Hounds, whose bloodlines are much admired by Elsie Morgan of the West Waterford Foxhounds in Ireland and by Ben Hardaway of the Midland Fox Hounds in America, plus several other Masters from different parts of the world.

It is not always true, however, and Leicestershire could belie the theory. The Cottesmore show tremendous sport with their modern foxhounds, which have quite a strong influence of Welsh blood and are well handled by their huntsman, Neil Coleman. Jerry Miller, Joint Master of the Iroquois Hunt in America, is a great admirer of these hounds and has much Cottesmore blood in his kennel.

One of the neighboring packs to the Cottesmore is the Belvoir. This pack also shows great sport in a similar country to the Cottesmore, well hunted by their huntsman Martin Thornton. Yet the pack consists of old English foxhounds. Very few American packs have used Belvoir blood, but their lines are now being sought after by many packs in England and Ireland.

The hills of Wales resound to the great cry of the Welsh hounds. These bloodlines are much sought after by Captain Ian Farquhar, Joint-Master and huntsman of the Duke of Beauforts Hounds. Ian's father, Sir Peter Farquhar, also admired the Welsh blood. It may interest you to know that Sir Peter Farquhar has been quoted as saying that he wanted to breed a pack of hounds that would hunt unassisted.

Lord Daresbury, when Master of the Belvoir and County Limerick Foxhounds, hunted old English hounds and his goal was the same as Sir Peter's. I think both of them achieved their aim, but with different types. In the Rolling Rock Country in Pennsylvania, the hounds certainly have to do it themselves. They are only seen when they cross a trail!

There is no doubt that Ben Hardaway is the champion of the Crossbred hound. He imported much blood from England and Ireland to his Midland Hounds, and it must be very rewarding to him to see the Midland bloodlines flowing through many kennels in England now.

One question you may have been asked by one of your non-hunting friends is, "Why have so many hounds to hunt one fox?" You put this question to the huntsman and his reply was that a pack of hounds should be like a good army regiment: well disciplined, but full of specialists. Some hounds are expert at finding foxes; you have seen one hound in your hunt's pack that is always drawing every place that a fox is likely to be lying. Other hounds as you have seen are good to

The true huntsman's friend is the experienced hound with "fox sense."

take the line up a road or on plough land. Some are experts over foiled ground, others have the ability to run at the head of the pack at pace, yet still be able to turn with the fox without losing momentum. Others are great marking hounds when the fox has gone to ground. Then there are the true huntsman's friends: those experienced hounds that possess what is known as "fox sense." These hounds at a check know through experience what a fox has probably done or where he is if he has tried to elude the pack by climbing into a derelict building or hiding in a dry ditch. There are also hounds known as pack hounds; these are the ones that add cry to the pack, and every pack should have a good cry.

You will realize as you sit toying with these thoughts that there are tremendous differences in weather conditions in England, Ireland, and America. It is not always the terrain that hounds hunt over that should be considered, but also the scenting conditions that they must regularly have to hunt under. It has been a good day and, on the whole, a good season, and as it plays through your mind you realize that you have added a whole new dimension to your sport by taking a more lively interest in the hounds. You are determined that next season you will build upon what you have learned this year, and you resolve to keep a journal of what you see each day that you are out.

SIX

WHAT IS THE FOX DOING?

You're vermin to a vast of folk, but glory to few,
What is it, in your creeping stride that calls and
    calls and calls?
What is it, when the racing pack runs from
    scent to view?
That rallies us to ride our best—dead straight—
    and chance the falls.

—Will H. Ogilvie

As you stand on the lawn watching your dog sniff about the shrubbery by the light of the moon, you hear a shrill yap come from the bottom of the garden. The dog lifts its head and looks in the direction of the sound. You sit down on the garden seat to listen, wondering if you will see the fox. It is a balmy spring evening, and as you sit your mind again turns to the day's hunting. This time it centers on the hunted fox. Disappointing for the huntsman not to have caught it, but for you and ninety-nine percent of the mounted field, you are not ever-worried. It was a good hunt over a good line of country. Anyway, it is very rare that a field member sees hounds catch a fox.

You hear a shrill yap.

It seems strange to you that the fox had taken so much finding by the pack, especially at the end of the season when all of the foxes in your country have been well hunted. Perhaps it was the fact that he had been hunted before that he was loath to leave the covert. Or perhaps it was because he hunts by scent himself that he knew scent would be good today and that he would have a job to evade the pack. Therefore he clung to the covert until Wagtail proclaimed his presence.

You have often heard of hounds drawing over a fox in covert. This is not always the hounds' fault; it is often caused by the huntsman being in too much of a hurry. Today the huntsman did not worry about the mounted field, even though you heard one of the professional horsewomen in the field grumbling over the long wait. He had that gut feeling that somewhere in the covert his hounds would find a fox. He gave his hounds time. After drawing it through the first time, he had the good sense to try back through it again, which proved successful.

EVASIONS

A fox, as you know, will cling to the covert if it has one or two of its kind with it, trying to pass the baton and slip away while the pack is hunting one of its comrades. Perhaps you do not know that foxes do not like terribly thick covert. They like the type of covert that is warm and out of the wind and one in which they can move about quickly if disturbed. Foxes do not like coverts that are frequented by flocks of starlings making much noise and a lot of droppings. Nor do they like broom when the seed shells are popping. Coverts that have been laid (i.e. cut down to make undergrowth) will not hold foxes until they have settled and stopped cracking with the wind.

You think back to when the fox ran the road. Why did he do that? Many times while driving at night you have seen a fox in your car headlights crossing a road, but you have never picked up a fox in your lights either running toward you on a road or running away from you. One can only assume that the fox has run the road because it is good going or perhaps, having hunted a hare fruitlessly up a road himself, he is aware that it leaves little scent.

We cannot say that it leaves no scent, however, as you saw that good dog, "Waggoner," took the line up the road. There is no doubt that foxes wander along the trails in woods. Presumably they do this to pick up the scent of rodents that may have crossed over. It is always a worry to a huntsman when a fox has run a quiet country road as to how far he has run it. This is why road-running hounds such as Waggoner are so important to a huntsman. He has to trust them implicitly.

You noticed the artificial manure and you obviously noticed the natural manure, both of which caused hounds to check, but one cannot reason that the fox ran over these to obliterate the scent. Presumably the fox had many nocturnal wanderings over these fields, and it was just his way of passage. It was perhaps the same when the fox became involved with the deer. It may not have been intentional, as the deer may have been behind the fox, but you do know that a fox will often run a deer *trace* because the going is good. Also you have often seen a hare run through the same *smeuse* in a fence as the fox. To them it is just a natural gateway. It is under these circumstances that not only the huntsman has to trust his hounds, but also the whippers-in have to be very cautious about shouting "ware riot."

Whether the hunted fox today was trying to pass the baton onto the fresh fox in the rough fields you do not know. The main body of the pack did not deviate from a straight line. On another day you did see a brace of foxes in front of the pack, as did the huntsman who cracked his whip behind them. With this the foxes separated, and the pack settled on one to provide a good hunt, with the quarry being caught at the end.

A fox will often run a deer trace because the going is good.

You reflect on the hounds at the entrance to the drain when the fox had evaded the pack in the hedgerow. At the end of the day you had questioned the huntsman about this incident. He explained to you that he thought it was more than likely there was a vixen with cubs in the drain. It would be very unusual for a fox to enter an earth or drain under those circumstances. He has known it to happen, but it is a very rare thing.

Even with a well-stopped country,[3] a fox out of his area will often run over an open earth or drain. Perhaps he is not familiar with these places of refuge, or perhaps he is not hard-pressed enough to take refuge in them. Also, as we noted, if it is the time of year when a vixen is below ground

3. A well-stopped country refers to hunting countries where *earth stopping* is practiced. It is not practiced in North America. However, in England, where foxes are numerous and destructive, many farmers insist that foxes be killed by the hunt. In those countries, the entrances to active earths are *stopped* (covered) the night before a hunt, while the foxes are above ground, to prevent them from going to earth when pressed by hounds the next day.

with her cubs, a fox will not enter the place unless extremely hard pressed.

Despite what the opposition to hunting may think, huntsmen and terrier men are some of our most knowledgeable naturalists. One who is known the world over for his knowledge of foxes, otters, deer, and badgers is Charles Parker, the long-time terrier man to Captain Wallace and Captain Evan Williams (Master and huntsman of the Tipperary, Ireland, from 1953 to 1971).

In the course of conversation the terrier man tells you of a vixen that had her cubs up in the thick growth of a lime tree. At Moore's Fort in the Scarteen Foxhounds' country in Ireland, a vixen reared her cubs, in a lime tree every year. The terrier man went on to tell you that most huntsmen prefer to have *stub-bred* cubs, as they are generally stronger than those born below ground and less prone to go to ground when hunted.

You have come to realize that the best or longest hunts have often taken place in January and early February during the *clickitting* season. Dog foxes have traveled long distances to find a mate and when disturbed by hounds will return to their home country. The first traveling dog fox you saw was a couple of seasons ago. Hounds had found him in a fence just outside a covert where he had kenneled for the day. Presumably the vixen was in the covert. The fox had run straight past the mounted field, and you noticed that he looked very wet and black even though the day was dry. A dog fox that has been clickitting is very easy to identify. Also at this time of the year, dog foxes are often chopped quickly as they are tired.

SCENT

The huntsman has already explained to you that a *heavy vixen* carries very little scent. Now you recall when, earlier in the season, you had seen cubs, but the hounds did not appear to be able to hunt them. Then, all at once, the cry increased and hounds ran hard. The reason for this was not a tremendous change in scenting conditions, said the huntsman, but the pack had changed onto an old fox. Cubs give off little scent; it is nature's way of protecting them. The same thing happens in the spring of the year when heavy vixens are afoot; they, too, give off little scent.

"Scent is a very incomprehensible, uncontrollable phenomenon, constant only in its inconsistency," said Mr. Jorrocks. Your huntsman has told you that there is always some idiot that comes up to him at the meet and tells him that scent will be good. It is only the fox and the hounds that know how the scent will be lying. The huntsman will not be sure until he has perhaps found his second fox, as foxes, like *homo sapiens*, all smell different.

Another cause of frustration for a huntsman is when a member of the field tells him that he or she can smell the fox. This generally is a sign of a poor scenting day as the scent has risen up well above the hounds' heads. Or perhaps it is when a dog fox has marked his territory the night before. There are many theories of why scent should be good and why it should be poor. Your huntsman will again tell you that most of these theories have been proved wrong. One incident comes to mind: before moving off from a cubhunting meet in Limerick, Percy Durno, who had found fame as huntsman at the Heythrop and later as Captain Wallace's kennel huntsman, pointed at the *gossamer* (filmy cobwebs) that lay thick on the ground, saying, "There will be no scent today with those on the ground." Hounds found, and that was the last we saw of them. The only way we could tell where they had gone was by following their tracks through the gossamer.

You are aware that November is a notoriously bad scenting month due to the fallen leaves, and scent remains poor until a fall of rain settles the leaves. You may have noticed that there is very little scent when the tips of the hounds' sterns are covered in blood, but you may have also discovered that there is a scent before a hard frost or before a snowfall. Other than that, scent remains a mystery to you as it does to any other normal-minded hunting person!

Thinking back to the day's hunting and some of those days earlier in the season, you wonder why the hunted fox had run along the top of the dry stone wall. Did he do it because it was easier than running through the gorse? Or did he do it because he thought it would obliterate his scent?

It seemed pretty obvious that day in March when the fox ran through the flock of sheep that he was trying to foil his scent; or was it just by chance that the sheep ran up together to cross his line? You and many other sportsmen and women give these things a lot of thought. Perhaps even the huntsman and terrier man cannot truthfully give a reliable answer why a fox does a certain maneuver.

Intentional or just chance? Perhaps even the huntsman cannot give a reliable answer as to why a fox does a certain maneuver.

In America there are grey foxes as well as the red fox. Some huntsmen are of the opinion that the grey carries a different scent than the red fox. Again, some huntsmen do not like hunting the grey fox as they are inclined to run in small circles and are also capable of climbing a tree in the same manner as a cat.

ETHICS

Oddly enough, one of the best hunts I have had in Rolling Rock was with a grey fox that provided the field with a three-mile point before giving up his brush. Thinking of foxes being caught by hounds you think back to your early years when you were not quite sure about the ethics of foxhunting. Now that you have enjoyed your hunting for several seasons you have come to realize that controlled hunting is a proven means of maintaining a healthy and vigorous population. With rare exceptions, it is the old, weak, or sick fox that is killed by hounds in North America.

In England and Ireland, where foxes are so numerous as to constitute a serious nuisance, foxhunting is a necessary and humane way of controlling the population. You understand that the fox lives by following the scent of smaller animals, and he not only kills for food but also kills for pleasure, particularly if he gets into a chicken or pheasant pen.

In areas of overpopulation, it is necessary for litters of cubs to be disturbed so that the fox population is not allowed to get out of hand. The fox hunted by a pack of hounds either escapes to run another day or dies an extremely quick death. It is incorrect to say that a fox is terrified all the time he is being hunted. You have seen how cooly and confidently he lopes along ahead of hounds. It is only at the very end, if he is run down, that he may feel fear. But even at the end there have been many cases of the fox turning to face the hounds. Your huntsman will tell you of many foxes that his hounds have caught that have either been maimed by the shotgun or have had the remains of a snare eaten into their necks. Then there was the old fox with no teeth in his head. Much better to die quickly than die a lingering death through wounds or starvation.

You know that if hunting with hounds were to stop, there would be a serious decline in the health and vigor of the fox population. As foxes no longer have a natural predator, their population has to be managed and, in certain areas, controlled. It is all very well for some to say that nature will take care of itself. Perhaps it does, but mange is not a very pleasant thing to see in foxes, and it is considered by some knowledgeable people that mange only occurs in areas where there is an overpopulation of foxes.

Once again the fox yaps, and just as it comes toward you the dog sees it and takes off after it into the dark. Some people will tell you that foxes only bark when they are looking for a mate or when a vixen has lost her cubs. Lord Daresbury was adamant about this, but his kennel man, Tom Meehan, and that wonderful covert keeper at Kilmeedy in Ireland, Jerry Kelly, both disagreed with him. I kept an open mind until I went down to visit Trish and Christian Hueber at Indian Hill in Penn Valley, Pennsylvania, where much of this book was written. Trish feeds her foxes with the best of beef, broth, and also a measure of Ivomec deworming medication. As I sat writing, the foxes would run about the garden, chasing squirrels, chipmunks, and eating out of the bird feeders. The odd one would sit on the steps in the garden, and yap at the dachshunds trying to get them to play tag. Therefore, I can only presume that the fox in your garden this evening was doing the same to your dog.

The dog returns, and you stand up to go back inside the house. As you enter, the telephone rings. It is the Master. He wonders if you would like to visit the kennels tomorrow. He has noticed that you have taken a keen interest in the hounds, and he would like you to see what goes on during the *closed season*.

SEVEN

WHAT DOES THE MASTER DO?

The Master put old Roman by
And eyed the thrusters heedfully.
He called a few pet hounds and fed
Three special friends with scraps of bread.

—John Masefield

"No one is too good to be a Master of Foxhounds, if he be gifted with the average endowment of tact, administrative talent, power of penetrating character, and all other attributes that form the essential equipment of a successful public man, so much the better; but he should at least be reared in the atmosphere and tradition of country life, fond of sport for its own sake, a good judge of horses and hounds, and the possessor of a remarkably thick skin."

So wrote Lord Willoughby de Broke in his delightful tome, *Hunting the Fox*. Lord Willoughby speaks of the Master of Foxhounds as a male figure. However, in this modern day and age as you are aware there are not only female Masters, but many of them hunt hounds as well. Presumably lady Masters came to the fore during the Second World War. Mrs. Vernon Williams kept the Eridge Foxhounds going at this time, as did

Lady Helena Hilton Green at the Cottesmore in England. Her husband was the very famous amateur huntsman, Major "Chetty" Hilton Green.

In Ireland, Mrs. Pug Alexander hunted the County Limerick Foxhounds while her husband, Major John Alexander, was away on active service. Tony Tarry, ex-MFH of the County Limerick, tells the story of John Alexander and Paddy McCann when they were based in Italy together. One morning John Alexander appeared to be a little depressed. Paddy turned to him and said, "Don't worry John, we will soon be home." "It is not that," replied John. "It is the thought of that woman with my hounds!"

The indomitable Mary "Sister" Grew took over the Norfolk Hunt pack in Massachusetts for the duration of the war. Mrs. Grew, her drag man, and her kennel man all had young families at the time. On hunting days, the youngsters were put into the hound truck, which had a wire cage on the back, for safekeeping. Today, America has many more female Masters hunting their own hounds than does England or Ireland.

Lord Willoughby de Broke says that "no one is too good to be a Master of Foxhounds." Just fifty years later, near the turn of the twentieth century, Sir Gilbert Greenall was considered not quite good enough by the Cheshire in England and was turned down when he applied for the Mastership, because, being in the brewing business, he was classed as a tradesman! However, Sir Gilbert went on to serve as Master at the Belvoir for sixteen years. His son, the second Lord Daresbury, served as Master at the Belvoir for thirteen years before taking the County Limerick Foxhounds in Ireland. One of the reasons that he left the Belvoir was due to the fact that an amateur has never hunted the Belvoir, and Lord Daresbury wanted to hunt hounds.

The Master of Foxhounds, be it male or female, has much work to do not only organizing a day's hunting, but also organizing the whole hunting year, which starts on May 1 of each year and finishes on the last day of April the following year. In England, the Master is generally engaged by a committee that will guarantee so much a year to run the hunt on. Any deficit at the end of the year must be made up by the Master. It has been known for Masters not only to run the hunt off the guarantee, but also to live off the guarantee. Nowadays some of the bigger packs in England pay the Master to hunt the hounds and run the country.

There are no Masters left in England who hunt their own hounds, as did the Tenth Duke of Beaufort. He was the last Master and huntsman of a ducal pack belonging to the family. Even for an amateur, especially the Duke of Beaufort who had a whole host of public duties to perform, hunting hounds four days a week and organizing the country was and is hard work. This is why many amateur huntsmen have a Joint Master. The Joint Master may or may not help financially, but he or she will help in running the country.

When Lord Daresbury hunted the County Limerick Foxhounds he had my father-in-law, Mr. Tony Tarry, as his Joint Master. Mr. Tarry's job was to look after the farmers and sort out any problems that occurred during the course of a day's hunting. He missed many good hunts by staying behind to pacify a farmer who had been upset by the hunt passing through his land. Being a qualified veterinary surgeon was a great bonus, and this was brought to the fore during a very famous hunt in Limerick.

Lord Daresbury and his bitches had found a fox in the Meat Factory Bog at Rathkeale and hunted it to the Doohyle at Cappagh. From here it turned back and ran through Stoneville where hounds checked. It was here that Mr. Tarry noticed a sheep with a prolapsed uterus. Jumping off his horse and handing it to a field member, he removed his coat, caught the sheep, put the uterus back, and was back on his horse just as hounds re-found the line. The pack went on to catch their fox at Ardagh, having made a seven-mile point.

Some hunts have several Joint Masters who all have their own duties to fulfill. One may be put in charge of the horses, the other the breeding of the hounds, the others may have their own section of hunt country to look after. Some Masters prefer to have area managers instead of a Joint Master. These managers are generally members of the hunt. They look after an area of hunt country, including the erection of hunt jumps, and are responsible for farmer relations in that area. There may also be a shooting plantation or preserve to complicate matters.

The committee engages the Master, but it is the Master who is responsible for the hiring and firing of the hunt staff. Notice of disengagement should be given no later than February 1 on either side. This gives staff personnel and hunts at least three months to secure positions or engage personnel before the new hunting year starts on May 1.

If a Master hunts hounds himself he will have a kennel huntsman who is responsible for the running of the kennels and the care of the hounds. The kennel huntsman will also whip-in to the Master on hunting days. If the Master is absent for some reason then the kennel huntsman will hunt the hounds. If the hunt establishment is large, a second whipper-in will be engaged. Sadly nowadays, a professional second whipper-in is a rare thing.

A kennel man is employed to look after things at home on a hunting day. Again, a large establishment may have a second kennel man, but second kennel men, like second whippers-in, are an endangered species. The Master may also have a groom or grooms depending on how many horses are kept. Obviously a large establishment hunting four days a week will require more hounds and more horses than a pack hunting two days a week.

If you have the good fortune to be hunting with a well-established hunt, your Master has been at the head of affairs for many seasons. He or she has devoted much time to the breeding of the hounds. Over the years a pack of hounds has been bred that not only are goodlooking in every way, but are celebrated for showing good sport. This has required a great deal of research into the *Foxhound Kennel Stud Book* and many visits to hound shows and puppy shows. Your Master has invested much of his time into your hunt.

His attention to detail in running the country and organizing hunting days is well known. He spends time in the summer months exercising hounds with his huntsman and visiting landowners and farmers. He does his best to buy straw, hay, and oats from within his hunting country.

The Master spends time in the off-season exercising hounds
with his huntsman and visiting landowners and farmers.

If your Master is like most, he lives for his hunting, but he retains a professional huntsman. He has never wanted the pressure of hunting hounds. He just wants to enjoy his hunting and watch his hounds work. For the same reason, he often has a hunt member as Field Master. But he is also aware that his Field Master knows every inch of the country and the name of every farmer and landowner. Therefore he can trust him implicitly with a large mounted field crossing the country.

The Master, as you know, is at the head of affairs. It is not an enviable position. He has many decisions to make, particularly to the state of the land before a hunting day. He may consider the land to be too wet to hunt, too hard with frost, or too deep with snow. Whatever decision he makes, it will not always be popular with every member of the hunt. If he considers the land to be too wet he is thinking of his landowners; if it is frozen or under deep snow he is thinking of his hunt staff horses.

He also has to hunt the country "fairly," meaning that he has to cover all of his country without over-hunting one part, while under-hunting perhaps not such a fashionable piece of country. This sometimes causes comment from hunt members, but the Master has the interest of his landowners and the country as a whole at heart and should not be criticized.

Through the entire hunting season, which generally starts with autumn hunting in August or September and continues on into March, the Master is on call seven days a week. It is all very well saying that he or she can delegate; a good Master will do this. But there are occasions when the Master has to be in attendance to overcome the problem. A landowner who has had his property abused by the hunt or has some other grievance obviously likes to see the man at the top, and quite rightly looks on it as a mark of disrespect if the Master does not visit him in person.

It is generally accepted that a Master has more problems during a good season than a bad one. Staff horses work harder and therefore may not come out of the stable so regularly, leaving the staff short of horses. More country is crossed and therefore more damage is done to fences. This gives him more landowners to visit. In a good season, your Master's telephone never stops ringing. Hopefully some of the calls will be from hunt members thanking the Master for a good day, but this is not always the case. It is more likely a landowner or farmer with a grievance against the hunt.

Besides having a loyal hunt staff, the Master must have a chairman who backs him up all of the time and a committee that is made up of genuine hunting people. Only those who hunt regularly in the field can fairly judge the Master's performance.

You have long been aware of the enormous amount of work your Master does in the interest of your sport, but it is good to review it periodically as we have done here. Hopefully you have been reminded of some of the problems that your Master has to deal with, and you realize that he or she has earned the full support of every member.

EIGHT

THE KENNEL

O'er all let cleanliness preside, No scraps
Bestrew the pavement and no half picked
    bones
To kindle fierce debate or to disgust
That nicer sense on which the Sportsman's
    hope
And all his future triumphs must depend.

—Edith Somerville

You are eager to visit the kennels, and you arrive a little before the appointed hour. As you turn into the kennel drive you see the head groom turning a couple of horses out into a paddock. You are aware that he has worked for a good many years at the hunt stable as stud groom, but you have never met him. He is one of the unsung heros of the hunt, with the great responsibility of turning out the hunt horses fit and sound three or four days a week. He starts early in the morning and finishes late—a "back room boy"—but a very important member of the hunt staff. He waves cheerfully as you slow down to pass him.

On reaching the kennel area you park your car, and as you close the door the huntsman walks across to greet you.

At this moment the hounds start to *sing* in the kennel. The huntsman explains to you that they have heard the Master's truck turn into the kennel drive. It is incredible how hounds recognize the engine of certain cars. Even after Major Field Marsham had retired from hunting the Eridge Foxhounds, those hounds would still sing when they heard his old Ford van turn into the kennels. The hounds at the Heythrop that had been left at home on a hunting day would sing when they heard the hound van coming home, even if it was three miles away. If I leave a hound out during a day's hunting at Rolling Rock and go back to look for it in my Subaru, nine times out of ten the hound will come to the sound of the car engine.

The Master greets you enthusiastically as he gets out of his truck, and the huntsman leads the way to the kennels. As you follow him you admire how neat and tidy the grounds are around the kennel, but once inside the kennel you are amazed at the cleanliness and lack of odor. Naturally there is a doggy smell, but there is not a smell of *"pure."*

Many years ago at the Limerick kennels it was the second kennel man, Jack Dwyer, who had the unenviable job of loading the pure onto a horse and cart. He would then deliver it to a local farm where it was spread on the land. One morning he met the parish priest who used to ride his horse visiting his parishioners. He greeted Dwyer and asked him what he had in the cart. (The priest obviously did not have a "good nose.")

Dwyer replied, "Pure, Father."

"What do you mean, 'pure,' Dwyer?"

"Pure sh-t," answered Dwyer.

As you follow the huntsman and Master you are greeted with a friendly smile and handshake by the first whipper-in. The Master informs you that hounds are to be walked out, and he hands you a length of plastic pipe so that you can prevent the more friendly members of the pack from jumping up on you. The hounds are waiting eagerly on the draw yard, and with a signal from the huntsman the first whipper-in opens the door. The hounds stream out with boisterous pleasure to dance around the huntsman. Meanwhile the first whipper-in has quickly put himself in a position in front of the pack, making sure that one or two of the more exuberant do not go too far beyond the bounds of discipline.

You are interested to see that the huntsman does not carry any biscuits in his kennel coat pockets. He does not have to buy the pack's love. The hounds respect him and love him for being the "doggy" man that he is.

As the hounds settle, you walk with the Master and he explains to you how foxes are caught in the kennel. For a second you wonder what he is getting at; surely foxes are not brought to the kennel to be fed to the hounds! No, the Master continues by telling you how essential it is to have a well-bred, well-made, and fit pack of hounds. All that is accomplished in and around the kennel, even before hounds ever get their first smell of a fox.

There is a quote from an old huntsman that "you breed for work and get them as good looking as you can." The Master explains to you that longevity is important in a pack. A hound that is built physically correctly will be able to continue hunting longer than one that has faults. As a result, that hound will become more experienced in hunting the fox on different scenting days, thereby gaining fox sense and, hopefully, passing that sense on to some of the younger hounds.

Voice has a great deal to do with hunting a pack of hounds, also. The Master tells you that it is very easy to lose the cry. A hound running mute in front of a pack of hounds can soon ruin the cry. Major Russell, when Master and huntsman of the Waterford Hounds (Ireland) used to carry a list of the young hounds during cubhunting. His kennel huntsman also carried one. When either of them heard a young hound's voice they put a tick against its name. At the end of the cubhunting season they compared their lists. Any hound that was not ticked was drafted. Needless to say the Waterford Hounds had great voices.

Lord Daresbury, when Master and huntsman of the Country Limerick Foxhounds, would not hunt a hound that was over four seasons. He showed tremendous sport, but I must say that when I took over the hounds I kept an older pack because I valued the experience of the older hounds.

The Master tells you that he was extremely lucky to take over a first-class pack of hounds that had been bred on the same lines for a quarter of a century. He goes on to explain that it was not easy to keep the standards of the pack high. He and his huntsman worked together, not only to keep the pack even and full of quality, but also to maintain the working quality of the pack. Lord Willoughby de Broke considered that it is far easier to raise the fortunes of a pack that had fallen into a slough than it is to maintain a brilliant pack at a consistently high level.

The Master continues by saying that he spends hours researching his stud books and visiting many kennels in the summer months in search of a stallion hound or perhaps a brood bitch. He tells you of a stallion hound that he sent to another pack that was hunted by an amateur. The hound would do nothing in the field for this huntsman, although it was brilliant at home. It was returned to its home kennel where it hunted in great style. The hound was then sent to a pack, this time hunted by a professional. Here it hunted as well as it did at home. The professional thought so much of this dog that your Master had a job getting him back once his stud duties were over.

You question the Master about this statement, asking if he thinks a professional huntsman was better than an amateur. The Master replies by saying that it was not unusual for a visiting stallion hound not to hunt for the huntsman of another pack whether he was professional or amateur, although he obviously preferred a visiting stallion hound that worked well with his pack. As a rule, he continues, professional huntsmen who have dedicated their lives to hounds and foxhunting *should* be better that the average amateur. However, it must not be forgotten that there have been many amateurs who have not only dedicated their lives to foxhunting but also invested a lot of their money into it. One such was Lord Daresbury at the County Limerick in Ireland. He led the life of a professional huntsman: he exercised his hounds, fed his hounds, and often cleaned his kennel. In America, Ben Hardaway and Jerry Miller would not be far behind him in their total dedication.

Luke Freeman, who was Lord Egremont's huntsman, was reputed as saying to his Master's son, "Stoody! Stoody! Stoody! Always stoodying at thy books. Take, I say, my advice, sir, and stoody foxhunting." Continuing, the Master explains that breeding foxhounds is a science. Many Masters have different ideas, but basically they are all looking for the same result: a pack that shows good sport under varied scenting conditions in varied climatic conditions.

There was a time when an individual hound could be identified as coming from a particular pack. Three examples of this were the Tynedale (UK) when under George Fairbairn's Mastership; Mr. Goshen's hounds, which are now defunct; and the Dumfriesshire, which sadly disbanded due to the ban on hunting in Scotland. There are examples of this today, but limited perhaps to the Scarteen foxhounds in Ireland and the Orange County hounds in America. Obviously the Old English foxhound is different from the modern foxhound, but one would have a job to say which kennel a certain Old English hound came from. Tom Sebright, the celebrated huntsman of the Fitzwilliam foxhounds in the nineteenth century, was quoted to have said, "Ah, my Lad! The Dam is the Secret." Many of the great hound breeders agree with this statement and pay much attention to the tail female lines in their kennel.

Following on with the pack you see on your left in another paddock two large wooden boxes placed well apart. You also notice the figure standing beside one of the boxes holding up the lid and recognize him as the second whipper-in. The Master explains that the boxes are small kennels, puppy boxes. When the brood bitch has whelped, she and her litter are placed in one of these boxes and bedded down with the best of oat straw. Here the brood bitch has complete freedom to come and go as she wishes until the whelps are weaned. The second whipper-in is cleaning out the boxes and moving them onto a fresh area.

You ask the Master how many times a day the pack is exercised, and he explains that it depends on the time of year. As the hunting season has just finished, the pack will be walked out twice a day. The young hounds, due to be entered

The brood bitch has freedom to come and go as she wishes,
to and from the puppy box, until the whelps are weaned.

in the following season, will slowly learn pack discipline this way. As the summer draws on and thoughts of cubhunting loom up, the pack will be exercised either with bicycles or horses. Your Master states that he prefers to exercise on the horses, but that is only his opinion. It is because of different methods in feeding, breeding, exercising, and hunting that whipper-ins move about during their apprenticeship. In this way they can learn different methods and come to their own conclusions of how things should be done. Then, when they eventually gain a huntsman's position, they can go about their business with confidence.

Summer exercise, continues the Master, was a very important time of the year. It was not only a time to get hounds fit, but a time to upgrade the young hounds' pack discipline. He also points out that it was a relaxing way for him to see what was going on in the country and also provided him with a chance to visit a landowner or puppy walker.

You have enjoyed walking with the hounds. You are also pleased that you recognize Wagtail and Villager. The huntsman has turned back toward the kennel. It is time for him to feed his hounds. As the pack reaches the kennel they are guided back into the draw yard. It is here that you meet the kennel man. Like the stud groom, you have heard about him but have not met him. He is another "back room boy," yet in the kennel he is second in command to the huntsman. Like the huntsman and whipper-in, he had to serve an apprenticeship, starting as kennel boy, then as a second kennel-man before becoming first kennel man. The Master, having introduced you, praises him as the best that you will find anywhere in hunt service. He is the most loyal of men, not only to the Master but also to the huntsman.

While the hounds were being walked out, the kennel man had been preparing their food. The Master points out that the pack is fed only once a day. Perhaps one or two older hounds or sick hounds are fed again later in the day. He continues by telling you that as with everything else, different huntsmen prefer different diets for their hounds. Some huntsmen, such as Bill Lander, who had a distinguished career as kennel huntsman to Captain Wallace at the Heythrop and then huntsman to the Wynnstay, prefer to feed raw flesh, claiming that not only is it great to put condition on a hound, but the bones clean their teeth, and, more importantly, hounds build up muscle in their shoulders pulling at the flesh. Others, such as the late Charlie Wilkin, who also hunted the Wynnstay, and Cooper Atkinson, who hunted the Brocklesby, claim that cooked feed is the best and cleanest.

In America most packs feed kibble, and here again huntsmen have their own opinions. Some prefer to soak it with water; others like to feed it dry; some like to mix it with

The huntsman must know his hounds: those that are gross feeders, those that are not so quick, and those that are delicate.

chicken necks. Whatever the diet, the Master tells you that a lot depends on whether the huntsman is a good feeder. The huntsman must know his hounds: those that are gross feeders, those that are not so quick, and those that are delicate.

You watch as the huntsman draws the delicate hounds out to be fed first. As they feed you are again impressed by the discipline: no fighting. Next the huntsman draws those a little heavier, and lastly he lets on those that would eat an elephant.

While all this is going on the Master is explaining to you that it is the care of the hounds that produces good sport: a strict worming program, exercise, nourishing feed, cleanliness in kennel, pack discipline. It all adds up. Any pack of hounds can run well on a good scenting day. It takes a good pack to show sport in moderate or poor scenting conditions.

He also talks to you about the welfare of lame hounds. Obviously during a day's hunting the pack traverses all kinds of terrain, and often a hound will return home lame either from a cut, a sprain, or perhaps a thorn in a toe. A good huntsman will know how to deal with these problems, but it is a great advantage to have a kennel man who is also well versed in the matters of lame hounds. He will be able to tend to them on hunting days when the huntsman is not at home.

The Master also explains to you that a huntsman has not only to get his hounds fit and in good condition for hunting, but also the more difficult job to keep them fit and in condition if they are laid off work due to frost or snow. It is all very well trying to put condition on a thin hound, but it is very difficult to take weight off a fat hound without breaking its constitution.

The hounds are fed, and it is time to take your leave. You thank the huntsman and then turn to thank the first whipper-in. Sadly it is also good-bye. Don't forget he is leaving shortly to go as huntsman to another pack of hounds. You shake his hand, pressing a folded bill into it, and wish him well for the future.

The Master walks you back to your car. On reaching it he takes you by the hand and congratulates you. Last night there had been a hunt meeting, and you had been proposed as a member by one of your friends and seconded by the hunt secretary. You are obviously thrilled. Now, in accordance with your hunt's pratice, you are entitled to wear a scarlet coat with the hunt collar and buttons. What a compliment! You thank the Master for such an entertaining morning and also for the good news.

As you drive home, you think of the honor that has been bestowed upon you. On numerous occasions you have spoken about membership with members of other hunts. Some hunts, you discovered, take you straight away as a member providing that you pay the correct subscription. Others, like your hunt, vote a member in. Other hunts have members, but they are not allowed to wear their colors until they are presented to them by the Master.

You are excited about next season and wonder if you will be allowed to wear your colors when you visit your neighboring pack. Some packs allow colors to be worn when visiting, others prefer visitors not to. No matter; you are now a full-fledged member of your home pack.

Just be cautious. You may, as a member, be persuaded to *walk* (take home for socializing) a couple of hound puppies!

> The count of the years is steadily growing;
> The Old give way to the eager Young;
> Far on the hill is the horn still blowing,
> Far on the steep are the hounds still strung.
> Good men follow the good men gone;
> And hark! They're running!
> They're running on!

—Will H. Ogilvie

— Magnificent Dog Hound

SUGGESTED READING

Books lead Folks to other Lands,
Books bind Folks with Friendship's Bands.
Books tell Folks of Bygone Days,
Books bring Folks Tomorrow's Ways.

—Eileen Burkard Norris

"Tut, tut, I never read a book! You ought to know by now that no true foxhunter does."

So said Lt. Col. J. Gannon in John Welcome's lovely novel, *Mr. Merston's Hounds* (Herbert Jenkins, 1953).

I sincerely hope that you disagree with Gannon. Where would the Derrydale Press Foxhunters' Library be if foxhunters did not read books? Not only that, there is much to be gleaned from books on foxhunting.

As the verse above reads, "Books lead Folks to other Lands." Perhaps a foxhunter may think of this as other "countries," but nobody can illustrate hunting countries around the world better than Jim Meads, the veteran pedestrian cameraman. His books, *They Still Meet at Eleven*, *They Will Always Meet at Eleven*, *My Hunting World*, and *In Full Cry*, create a wonderful kaleidoscope of hunting countries throughout the world of foxhunting. Jim Meads' books illustrate hunting with over four hundred packs of hounds! Obviously not all of these were foxhound packs, but he has visited most of them. These books give a wonderful visual insight.

To learn more about the hunting countries, you could do no better than to read *British and Irish Hunts*. These are written in three volumes by J.N.P. Watson. Watson wrote these books in the mid-nineteen-eighties with the idea of updating and perhaps replacing the huge tomes of the same name written nearly eighty years before. To get a good idea of the countries in America and Canada, one could not do better that to read Henry Higginson and Julien Chamberlain's work, *Hunting in the United States and Canada*. These books will not only give you a visual picture of the hunting countries, but they will tell you much of the people that were responsible for maintaining and promoting the various hunts. Hopefully, one day somebody will bring *Hunting in the United States and Canada* up to date. (Although Alexander Mackay-Smith did a great job in writing *Foxhunting in North America*.)

Speaking of Mr. Mackay-Smith, of his many literate offerings, *The American Foxhound 1747-1967*, remains the definitive work on the history of American hunting, the influential foxhound breeders, and the seminal bloodlines and types that constitute the modern American foxhound.

Perhaps to learn a little more about life in the hunting world, either as an amateur or professional, you will find these books of interest. Ben Hardaway's autobiography, *Never Outfoxed*, will tell you much about that most celebrated amateur huntsman of modern times in America. *Foxhunting with Melvin Poe*, written by Peter Winants, tells the story of a legend in his own lifetime. Poe earned fame as huntsman of the Orange County foxhounds in Virginia. Another well-written book giving some good insight into a famous American foxhunter who is no longer with us is *Try Back*, written by Henry Higginson. Higginson wrote several books, all of them worth reading. He also had the great honor of being the first American to judge at the Royal Peterborough Foxhound Show in England. At the time Higginson was Master of the Cattistock there.

To read about perhaps the most famous Master and huntsman of the twentieth century, you must have a copy of *Ronnie Wallace, The Authorized Version* by Robin Rhoderick-Jones. The name Wallace is revered all over the world where foxhunting takes place. He was a great breeder of hounds, and was also noted for his ability to organize a country for a day's foxhunting. Nothing was ever left to chance.

Another Wallace book is titled *Ronnie Wallace: A Manual of Foxhunting*, edited by Michael Clayton. This is a wonderful work that should be studied by every person that goes foxhunting. It is full of knowledge and good sense. In fact, Michael Clayton has written several books on the subject of foxhunting. All of them should be on your library shelf.

The Life of Frank Freeman by Guy Paget covers the career of one of England's finest professional huntsmen. Freeman has often been compared with Tom Firr, who hunted the Quorn from 1872 to 1899. Roy Heron wrote *Tom Firr of the Quorn*, another good biography of a professional huntsman.

Now let us take a look at some books that will give you an idea of the different types of foxhounds. Perhaps these books will also give you a little information about the science of breeding hounds. Of course there are *The Foxhound Kennel Stud Book*, published every year by the British M.F.H.A. and *The Foxhound Kennel Stud Book of America*, published each year by the American M.F.H.A. These books can trace a hound's pedigree back over two hundred years, but are compelling reading only for serious students of foxhound breeding.

Hounds of the World by Sir John Buchanan Jardine is a comprehensive study of the various breeds of hounds in England, America, and the Continent. It is also beautifully illustrated.

Daphne Moore's wonderful tome, *The Book of the Foxhound*, is superbly written and researched. This book will do much to help you understand how the foxhound has developed over the years. It will also show you several pedigrees of famous foxhounds of the last century. Also, *Hounds*, *The Modern Foxhound*, and *The Foxhound of the Future* are three titles written by C. R. Acton that are of interest.

Hunting by Scent by H.M. Budgett and *The Mytery of Scent* by H.B.C. Pollard will help you understand why hounds can run well on certain days and why they cannot on other days. Messrs. Budgett and Pollard have gone into great depths on the subject of scent. They are fascinating books, but I still agree with Mr. Jorrocks: "Constant only in its inconstancy! . . . There's nothing so queer as scent, 'cept a woman."

Well, you heard the fox bark at the bottom of the garden; and during the past few seasons you have seen many of them; but by reading Richard D. Clapham's books you will discover a great deal more about foxes. The two books I would recommend are *Fox, Foxhounds and Foxhunting* and *The Book of the Fox*. Clapham informs us about foxes in the lowland of England, foxes on the Fells, and foxes in North America. Both of these books are packed with information on scent, breeding, and habits.

Lionel Edwards' delightful book, *The Wiles of a Fox*, obviously well illustrated, shows how a fox is able to defeat a pack of hounds by using all kinds of cunning.

Perhaps the best book written in modern times about the fox and his environment is *The Fox and the Orchid* by Robin Page. Page does cover other mammals, birds, and fish, but it is all put together very well.

The Life of a Fox by Thomas Smith, who was Master of the Craven and later the Pytchley, tells the life story of several fictitious foxes. It is easy reading and very informative about the ways and habits of a hunted fox.

HYM, The Life of a Famous Fox by Cyril Heber Percy mixes fact and fiction about a famous Cottesmore fox that was hunted by the Cottesmore hounds for several seasons, giving the mounted field some great runs.

A very useful little book that will help you understand some of the hunting terms of the chase used by the hunt staff is *The Language of Sport* by C. E. Hare.

There have been many books written about hounds, hunting, and kennel management. Some would be quite hard going for the average field member, so I will endeavor to give you titles that will be of interest.

Peter Beckford's *Thoughts on Hunting* has often been called the huntsman's bible. To the more experienced huntsman it holds a wealth of knowledge and is truly a classic, but I often wonder if *Hunting the Fox* by Lord Willoughby de Broke would perhaps be more suitable for somebody like yourself, who has hunted a few seasons and wishes to learn more.

Mason Houghland's *Gone Away* is truly a super book for the American foxhunter to learn more about hunting in the kennel and the field.

Hounds and Hunting through the Ages by Joseph D. Thomas is a classic and well worth studying. Thomas draws some very good comparisons between hunting in America and

England. Ikey Bell's *A Huntsman's Log Book* and *Foxiana* are well worth reading. These two books hold a wealth of information. *Foxiana* is fiction, and if you enjoy fiction and wish to learn more about hunting in a lighthearted form, you could do no better than to read the books of R. S. Surtees, starting with *Handley Cross*. When you read these books you will discover that Surtees had incredible knowledge of foxhunting.

If you are looking for pure humor, then Edith Somerville and Martin Ross will amuse you endlessly with *Experiences of an Irish R.M.* and *Further Experiences of an Irish R.M.* The authors, Irish cousins, wrote many more titles just as good.

Continuing in the entertainment vein, Gordon Grand's *The Silver Horn* is a wonderful introduction to the classic stories and lovable characters created by this American foxhunter.

As you will have seen at the top of each chapter of this book, I have placed a verse of poetry. Most of these verses were taken from Will H. Ogilvie's *Scattered Scarlet*, which is well illustrated by Lionel Edwards.

In my opinion one of the best hunting poems ever written was "Reynard the Fox," or as it is sometimes called "The Ghost Heath Run." This poem was written by John Masefield.

If you disagree with the opinion of the fictitious Jig Gannon and would like to know still more about hunting books, we can once again return to the prolific Henry Higginson. His *British and American Sporting Authors* will be of great value to you.

These are just a few books that you may both learn from and be amused by.[4]

---

4. Out-of-print books on foxhunting are offered by Robin Bledsoe, Bookseller, 1640-BD Massachusetts Avenue, Cambridge, MA 02138; James Cummins, Bookseller, 699 Madison Avenue, New York, NY 10021; Hooper's Books, 1615 Eighth Street, NW, Washington, DC 20001; and Horse Country, 60 Alexandria Pike, Warrenton, VA 20186.

A good website for locating and purchasing out-of-print books is www .abebooks.com.

GLOSSARY

accounting for the fox	catching it or *marking* it to ground
all on	all hounds are present
bay	(verb) hounds bay at an earth when a fox has gone to ground, or at the base of a tree if a gray fox has climbed it
billet	fox droppings (also *scat*)
blank	fox is not found
brace of foxes	two foxes
brush	fox's tail
carrying a good head	when frontrunners in the pack run tightly abreast to pick up changes in the fox's direction (also *running with a good head*)
cast	a deployment of hounds trying to recover a lost line
check	when hounds lose the line of the fox
chop	(verb) hounds catch the fox while it is asleep, or nearly so
clickitting	when foxes mate or pair up
closed season	non-hunting season: late March through early August
cold nose	ability to detect very low levels of scent

cope	come, come on
couples	two leather collars joined by a chain
covert	(pronounced "cover"; the final "t" is silent) woods or thick brush where wild animals feel hidden and protected
cub	young fox
drag	the line the fox has traveled during his nocturnal perambulations
draw	deployment of hounds when searching for a fox
earth	underground hole (den or burrow) where foxes lie for protection
earth stopping	blocking entrances to fox earths at night while foxes are out hunting, so they cannot take refuge the next day
feather	(verb) the waving of a hound's stern when it detects and begins to follow the line of the quarry
foil	any scent that masks the fox's line, such as manure, cattle, sheep, fertilizer
full cry	when the entire pack is speaking on the line of the fox
gone away	hounds have left the covert and are running the line as a pack
gossamer	filmy cobwebs on the grass or bushes; more noticeable when there is a dew
headed	when the fox has been turned from its direction of travel by a car, person, or cur dog
heavy vixen	a female fox with cubs before whelping
heel line	the line of the fox opposite to the direction it is traveling
holloa	loud voice signal to huntsman and hounds that a fox has been viewed
honor	when hounds respect another hound's find and rush to its assistance

in whelp	pregnant
kennel huntsman	the hunt staff member responsible for the care of hounds in kennel and who whips-in to an amateur huntsman
leash of foxes	three foxes
leu in	huntsman's command to hounds to enter the covert and search for the fox
low scenting	describes a hound that can detect very low levels of scent
mark	(verb) by speaking and/or digging at an earth, hounds indicate that the quarry has gone to ground
mask	fox's head
open	(verb) refers to the first hound to speak to a line
pad	fox's foot
pure	hound excrement
riot	when foxhounds hunt anything but acceptable quarry
running with a good head	when front runners in the pack spread out to pick up changes in the fox's direction (also *carrying a good head*)
scat	fox droppings (also *billet*)
sing	when hounds hold their heads up and make a wonderful noise, often when they are happy. They should never be stopped from *singing* and should be allowed to finish their anthem
sink the wind	heading downwind
smeus	a run through a fence that may be used by fox, hare, rabbit, or other small animals
stern	hound's tail
stub-bred	foxes born above ground
tally ho	a term used when a fox is viewed in the open

tally ho, bike	a term used when a fox has been viewed going back into covert
tally ho, over	a term used when a fox is viewed over a trail or ride
thruster	a member of the mounted field who is out mainly to gallop and jump with little regard for what hounds are doing
trace	a track or path that deer use
un-kenneled	when the fox is roused from where he is lying
view holloa	screech shouted when fox is viewed, to let huntsman know a fox is afoot and to provide an audible beacon to which hounds may hark
vixen	female fox
walk	(verb) take foxhound puppies home for socializing
whelp	(noun) a hound puppy; (verb) to give birth